THE
ANGER
TOOLKIT

Quick Tools to
Manage Intense Emotions
& Keep Your Cool

MATTHEW McKAY, PHD • PETER D. ROGERS, PHD
RONALD POTTER-EFRON, PHD • PATRICIA POTTER-EFRON, MS
WILLIAM J. KNAUS, EDD • ALEXANDER L. CHAPMAN, PHD
KIM L. GRATZ, PHD

New Harbinger Publications, Inc.

Publisher's Note

Distributed in Canada by Raincoast Books

NEW HARBINGER PUBLICATIONS is a registered trademark of New Harbinger Publications, Inc.

Copyright © 2023 by Matthew McKay, Peter D. Rogers, Ronald Potter-Efron, Patricia Potter-Efron, William J. Knaus, Alexander L. Chapman, Kim L. Gratz
New Harbinger Publications, Inc.
5674 Shattuck Avenue
Oakland, CA 94609
www.newharbinger.com

Cover design by Amy Shoup; Acquired by Elizabeth Hollis Hansen; Edited by Brady Kahn

Library of Congress Cataloging-in-Publication Data

Names: McKay, Matthew, author. | Rogers, Peter D. (Peter Denny), 1941- author. | Potter-Efron, Ronald T., author.
Title: The anger toolkit : quick tools to manage intense emotions and keep your cool / Matthew McKay, PhD, Peter D. Rogers, PhD, Ronald Potter-Efron, PhD, Patricia Potter-Efron, PhD, William J. Knaus, PhD, Alexander L. Chapman, PhD, Kim L. Gratz, PhD.
Description: Oakland, CA : New Harbinger Publications, 2023. | Includes bibliographical references.
Identifiers: LCCN 2022036464 | ISBN 9781648481338 (trade paperback)
Subjects: LCSH: Anger. | Control (Psychology) | Self-help techniques. | BISAC: SELF-HELP / Self-Management / Anger Management (see also FAMILY & RELATIONSHIPS / Anger) | FAMILY & RELATIONSHIPS / Anger (see also SELF-HELP / Self-Management / Anger Management)
Classification: LCC BF575.A5 M367 2023 | DDC 152.4/7--dc23/eng/20220825
LC record available at https://lccn.loc.gov/2022036464

Printed in the United States of America

24	23	22								
10	9	8	7	6	5	4	3	2	1	First Printing

CONTENTS

Part 3: Getting Unstuck from Anger

Part 4: Being Good to Yourself

INTRODUCTION

These are extreme and uncertain times. From natural disasters to downsizing and automation to global pandemics that previously seemed unimaginable—not to mention political division about all of these things—we have more than enough to feel angry about.

By picking up this book, you are likely seeking relief from the burden of anger and the pain it causes you and others. Sometimes anger can be a helpful emotion, such as when it pushes you to stand up for yourself or others you care about or to advocate for a cause that you believe in. Other times, anger becomes intense and overwhelming and leads to urges to act in destructive or harmful ways. Often, anger is a response to pain, a way of coping when something feels very wrong or out of your control.

This book can help. The mental health tools contained in this anger management toolkit can give you a welcome respite from angry outbursts and resentments, so you can focus on finding calm in the here and now.

This short book compiles the easiest and most effective anger-reducing exercises, techniques, and practices from top mental health experts, all of whom have put these skills into practice with clients. In addition, the techniques come from evidence-based treatments. "Evidence-based" means not only that the tools in this book have worked for decades with hundreds of clients—they have—but also that they have been tested and approved in research labs all over the world.

Perhaps you have heard about cognitive behavioral therapy, dialectical behavior therapy, or neuroscience. If you have, then you might have a sense of how this book will help you. If you haven't, don't worry. Knowing about these therapies is not important when it comes to getting the most out of this book: improving your mood, getting a better understanding of your thoughts, and making sure that you are living in accordance with what really matters to you. If you are already interested in these therapies or if this book inspires your curiosity, you can explore these topics further in any number of books from New Harbinger Publications. We have suggested some supplementary reading at the back of the book.

You will first learn some techniques to reduce anger and hurtful actions toward yourself and others before you start on the more difficult work of managing the pain behind your anger. If you're able, work through this book from beginning to end, because it's easier to work on your anger once you've established a baseline of calm, or nonreactivity.

All of the techniques in this book can be used at a moment's notice—as needed and on demand. To get you what you need when you need it, you can begin using these techniques right away. For example, if a mindfulness exercise works well for you, go ahead and make it a habit before moving on to a new technique. The techniques are flexible enough to work with any kind of anger thought or feeling, so it's fine to jump in and out. Perhaps leaving the book on the coffee table—or somewhere else where it is readily available—can help you access relief when you need it. Keeping a journal will also help, especially with exercises that ask you to write things down.

As you move through the book, try to bring whatever amount of playfulness you can to these exercises and techniques. This can be tough when you're struggling. But do your best to keep an open mind. That said, if something doesn't feel like it's working for you, drop it and move on to something else. In these pages, you are the priority.

You also don't have to define yourself as a person with a "bad anger problem" to use this book. After all, everyone gets angry from time to time. Most of us get stuck at least once in a while, not knowing what to say or do with our anger. This book is designed to give readers with at least some anger problems quick and effective ways to manage their anger.

These truly are distressing times, but finding a moment to take care of your mental health doesn't have to be. With that…it's time to take a deep breath and turn the page.

PART 1

GET ANGER RELIEF RIGHT AWAY

Sometimes you need quick guidelines on how to defuse anger right away. Even though anger can be a helpful emotion, managing anger—especially when that anger is intense and overwhelming—can seem like an insurmountable goal. When people experience anger, they often have urges to act in ways that won't be effective and could actually make a situation worse. Do you notice that many of the urges associated with anger involve behaviors that are destructive?

One of the best things you can do when you're experiencing intense anger is to avoid acting on your urges. Not acting on your anger when you're most angry can protect you from some of the downsides of anger and keep you out of trouble. The emergency anger control skills in this section of the book are designed to help you avoid acting on intense anger and making things worse.

1: STOP BLAMING YOURSELF

What to Know

From the very start, it's important to get one thing straight: you aren't to blame because you struggle with anger. You are not a bad person because you've forgotten—perhaps repeatedly—all your resolutions to be cool and calm. Rather, you are a person in pain.

Often the roots of anger can be traced back to earlier times when you were hurt, abused, or neglected in your family of origin. The pain was something you carried, year after year. It may have left scars so that now it's hard to feel safe or loved or truly worthy. Sometimes it doesn't take much of a provocation to trigger those feelings of being unloved, unworthy, or unsafe—and the anger rises up right alongside that old pain.

Whether the pain is occasional or chronic, when it hits, it feels overwhelming. It's a wave that drives you into a state of mind where nothing matters but expressing what you feel. You shout it out, no matter who gets hurt or whatever the consequences.

Anger is a way of coping. It helps you, temporarily, to overcome the hurt and helplessness. For a moment you feel back in control, and that's exactly why anger is so hard to manage. If you try to put a cork in your anger, you may feel acutely the pain that triggered it.

So now is the time to stop kicking yourself. It doesn't help. In fact, blaming yourself for your anger simply creates more pain—bad, unworthy feelings—and the pain triggers more anger. It's a self-perpetuating cycle. First, recognize that your anger is:

- A response you learned early in life to cope with pain

- A way, however temporary, to overcome feelings of help-lessness and lack of control

- A habit that, up until now, you've lacked the tools to break

If you're going to get off this merry-go-round, you'll need another way to view your anger problem.

What to Do

When you get angry:

1. First, and most important, stop. Don't do or say anything. . Don't act on the angry feelings. This is just an emotion. It's a strong one, but you can feel it without turning it into behavior.

2. Try to step back from the feeling, and label it. Notice its strength: be aware of how it pushes you toward action. Accept it. There's nothing inherently wrong with anger. It's just a signal that you're in pain. The only problem is when you act on anger to hurt others or yourself.

3. Don't push the feeling away, but don't try to hold on to it either. It will come like a wave—building, cresting, then slowly receding. Let it come, and then let it go. Watch how it grows and diminishes, as if you were a scientist observing some interesting phenomenon. Take care not to do anything to amplify your anger. Don't dwell on the unfairness of the situation. Don't review past failings of the offending individual. Don't rehearse in your mind the events leading to your anger. Just notice and accept the feeling, watching as it gradually diminishes.

Remember, blaming yourself for your anger issues isn't going to solve anything or make you feel any less angry. Anger is a response to pain, and freeing yourself from blame and shame around your anger is an important step toward healing.

2: ANGER AND ITS COSTS

What to Know

Since you are reading this book, you probably realize your anger is creating problems, sometimes serious ones, in your life—and you're no longer minimizing the problem or in denial. Anger almost certainly has been causing problems for you and others, and it can be helpful to take a good look at where your anger or aggression may have messed up your life. Here are some possibilities:

- Your spouse, partner, or past partners: arguments, break-ups, physical violence

- Your children or stepchildren: useless fights, loss of love, loss of connection

- Your family of origin (parents, siblings): endless battles, cutoffs during which people won't talk with you, physical fights with brothers and sisters

- At work or at school: arguments with coworkers or school-mates, getting fired or suspended, failure to get promoted

- With the law: police calls, disorderly conduct charges, no-contact orders

- Your physical or mental health: increased anxiety or depression, anger-related accidents, high blood pressure

- Your finances: fines, replacing broken objects, attorney fees, cost of anger management programs

- Your values and spirituality: broken promises not to get angry or lose control, guilt and shame after blowups, anger at God

What to Do

Go through the items in the list to decide which areas of your life you most need to work on immediately. Please don't say "all of them," because that's probably too much to take on right now. Instead, be selective. Ask yourself this question: *Where is my anger causing the most friction, trouble, loss, and pain—both to myself and to others—right now?*

For instance, if your relationship with your twelve-year-old step-daughter is a disaster, and your anger is only making it worse, then make a commitment to quit getting angry at her, no matter what she says or does. Or maybe you're close to losing your job because of your cynical attitude. So for now, make a promise to yourself to keep those nasty thoughts and comments to yourself at work. That will buy you some time to change at a deeper level—to eventually quit thinking those mean-spirited thoughts and even start thinking more positive thoughts about your coworkers.

You and you alone are in charge of your anger. That's both good and bad, of course. It's good because you can take full responsibility for making your life better. It's bad because you can't blame others for your problems. The key question is what you will do with the behavior. Will you accept these anger invitations and react with anger, sarcasm, and aggression? Or will you pass on them, letting them go because they're not worth getting all upset over? You and you alone will make the decisions that determine how frequently you become angry and how much damage you do to yourself and others with your anger.

3: ACT THE OPPOSITE

What to Know

Have you ever noticed that your anger intensifies when you act in an angry way? People often say that yelling helps them blow off steam. But yelling is like barreling uncontrollably down a hill in a car and pressing on the gas instead of hitting the brakes. As you're yelling, your nervous system revs up, intensifying feelings of anger. Instead of blowing off steam, you're actually increasing your agitation. Acting on your urges when angry, such as yelling, creates a vicious cycle that can lead to disastrous consequences. Luckily, you can break the vicious cycle of anger by changing your actions.

One of the quickest ways to change a painful feeling is to act the opposite. Opposite action breaks the cycle of anger by directly modifying anger's behavioral component. By doing the opposite of your angry urges, you can reduce your anger and deal with it effectively, just as slowing down and gently applying the brakes can help you get a car under control. If you practice opposite action, you may discover that you can avoid consequences that make you angrier (such as conflict with other people) or lead to other negative emotions (guilt, shame, and sadness).

What to Do

1. Smile instead of frown. The very act of smiling when angry tends to diminish the strength of your upset feelings.

2. Speak softly rather than loudly. Go overboard on this. Make your voice lower and gentler than usual; try to make it soothing.

3. Relax instead of tighten. Let your arms hang loose. Take a breath. Lean against something in a casual way or sit with your legs crossed comfortably. Look calm even if you don't feel it.

4. Disengage rather than attack. You may want to get right in the other person's face. You may want to shake them—emotionally if not physically. Instead, look away or walk away. Make no comment about the provoking situation. Save it for another time. You'll only blow up if you try to deal with this now.

5. Empathize rather than judge. Say something mildly supportive, such as "This is a difficult situation for you" or "I can see why you're concerned [or upset, overwhelmed, dismayed]." It's okay if you don't feel supportive and the words seem phony. You can have a strong desire to take a two-by-four to the other person. But just *behave* as if you can appreciate their point of view.

Although the skill of opposite action might seem complicated at first, with practice it will start to feel more natural. With a lot of practice, you might find yourself using opposite action automatically, without much thought or effort.

More to Do

Opposite action tends to work best when you jump into it fully with body and mind (Linehan 1993a, 2015). You need to perform the action with your full attention. For example, if you are using the skill of empathizing rather than judging, this skill will be far more effective if you bring your full attention to the activity at hand. It can be useful to keep track of how mindful you are when you try an opposite action.

Pay attention to whether your mind is focused on what you are doing or if it's wandering somewhere else.

Afterward, consider whether you put your full effort into the opposite action. Were you giving it your full attention or were you doing it only halfway? Notice if you were doing an opposite action without your full attention. Then, the next time you're in a similar situation, you can remind yourself to really immerse yourself in the opposite action and to be fully present. See if you can tell any difference between doing the opposite action mindfully versus mindlessly. Was doing it mindfully more effective?

4: TAKE A GOOD TIME-OUT

What to Know

You are getting angry. You don't want to lose control and say or do something stupid. You need to get away. Here's what to do. Follow the four Rs so you can take a good time-out. The four Rs of a good time-out are: recognize, retreat, relax, and return.

Recognize: You need to recognize the early signs that you're beginning to lose control, so you can take a good time-out. Typically, these signals might include raising your voice, starting to pace, feeling hot as your blood pressure rises, realizing you're not able to listen to what others are saying, having aggressive thoughts and urges to act on them, making fists, feeling attacked, and so on. The message is "I better get out of here now, before I lose control."

Retreat: Go somewhere safe and quiet. Getting away will allow you to calm down so you can think better. A word of caution: don't go someplace where people will urge on your anger. The purpose of a retreat is to calm down, not rev up.

Relax: Let the anger drain out of your mind and body. You might want to exercise to help that happen. Or read a book. Or go fishing. Don't drink or use drugs, though. You'll probably make things worse instead of better that way.

Return: It's not enough simply to calm down. After you've regained your composure, you need to return, so you can try to resolve whatever issue triggered your anger. Note: If your fourth R is to run away instead of return, you aren't taking a good time-out.

What to Do

The time to plan your time-out is before you need to take one. Once you get angry, you may not be able to think clearly enough to do it right. Use the four Rs to develop a time-out plan.

Recognize: Write down five signs that you are losing control of your anger. If you can't think of five, ask your partner, family, and friends for help.

Retreat: Assume you're really angry and will need at least thirty minutes to calm down. Where can you go? How will you get there? What's your backup plan in case you can't go to this first place?

Relax: How will you go about letting the anger drain away? Will you go for a walk, do breathing exercises, distract yourself with work or activities, or talk with someone who won't throw fuel on your fire?

Return: You'll need to be willing to talk about what happened without blowing up again. How will you know when you can do that?

Remember, you shouldn't overuse your time-outs. Make sure to call for a time-out only when you actually need to take one. If you overuse time-outs, you'll lose credibility.

5: MINDFULLY ATTEND TO YOUR ANGER

What to Know

Mindfulness involves paying attention to, contemplating, and noticing something while letting go of judgments and assumptions. To mindfully attend to an experience, you must take a step back and look at it objectively without evaluating it as either good or bad or right or wrong. Don't try to change it. Instead, be open to the experience, regardless of whether you like or dislike it. This process is a lot like walking outside in the morning and paying attention to the weather—the warmth or coolness of the air, the clouds in the sky, even the feeling of rain—and not being attached to wanting anything to be different. When it comes to anger or anger-provoking situations, mindfully attending to them is much easier said than done.

What to Do

This exercise provides simple step-by-step instructions for mindfully attending to the components of your anger without judgment.

1. Find a comfortable and quiet place where you can sit or lie down.

2. Close your eyes.

3. Focus on your breathing. Notice what it feels like to breathe in and breathe out.

   Notice which parts of your body move as you breathe in and out.

4. Think about a recent time when you felt anger at a moderate level of intensity: try focusing on a time when your anger was around a 4 or 5 on a scale from 0 to 10, where 0 equals no emotion and 10 equals the most intense emotion possible. Focus on this experience and try to get a clear picture of it in your mind.

5. Bring your attention to your body and notice where in your body you feel the emotion. Scan your body from head to toe, paying attention to any sensations in your head, neck, shoulders, back, chest, abdomen, arms, hands, legs, and feet. Spend about ten seconds on each area of your body, stepping back in your mind and just paying attention to and noticing the sensations.

6. Once you have finished scanning your body, bring your attention to the parts of your body where you feel anger. Zero in on these sensations. Watch them rise and fall as you would watch a wave rising and falling in the ocean. Breathe in and out, just noticing the sensations, watching without judgment.

7. If you begin to label or judge the sensations, take note of your evaluation or judgment and then simply bring your attention back to noticing the sensations as mere sensations.

8. Bring your attention to any thoughts that are present, focusing on just noticing these thoughts as thoughts without attaching to them. If you find yourself getting caught up in your thoughts or judging yourself for having them, notice what's happening and then bring your attention back to simply noticing the thoughts that are present.

9. See if you can bring your attention to any action urges you are experiencing. Focus on just noticing these urges as they rise and fall, bringing attention to the ways they change or stay the same.

10. Keep focusing on the different components of your emotion without escaping or avoiding them. Continue to notice your sensations, thoughts, and action urges without trying to push them away or change them. Do this for about ten to fifteen minutes or until the emotion subsides and you no longer feel angry.

Practicing this exercise will help you respond mindfully in anger-provoking situations.

6: REPLACE NEGATIVE THOUGHTS WITH POSITIVE ONES

What to Know

Angry people are awfully good at thinking negatively about what others say and do. Here's a way to change that pattern of thinking. Classic cognitive behavioral therapy (CBT) begins with these thoughts:

1. Events just happen.

2. We humans create meaning for events.

3. That meaning can be negative, positive, or neutral.

When angry, you likely create far more negative meaning for events than helpful, leading to unnecessary hostile actions or remarks. But you can learn to change your thinking from negative to positive and in this way avoid habitual anger. Here's the technique you need to make this change:

1. An event occurs.

2. You notice you are automatically making a negative interpretation of it (which would normally lead to you saying or doing something hostile).

3. Instead, you choose to make a more positive (or at least neutral) interpretation of the event, which leads you to respond with less anger or hostility.

Here's an example:

A guy is driving at 55 mph in a 55 mph lane. You think, "He's slowing me down. What a moron!" You would normally blow the horn, give him the finger, and stay mad for an hour or more. Instead, you catch that negative thought and replace it with "I'm not in a hurry, so why get upset?" You calm down and wait patiently for a good opportunity to pass him.

What to Do

Think of one recent situation in which you became angry. Would this method have helped you respond any differently? See if you can use this method to change how you would react to the same situation the next time it occurs.

7: BREATHING AND RELAXING IN STRESSFUL SITUATIONS

What to Know

One of the best ways to lessen anger is to learn how to breathe and relax in stressful situations. You will need to practice this technique regularly for it to be useful, though. Fortunately, it feels really good to be able to let go of your anger just by altering your breath.

What to Do

Practice your deep breathing:

1. Find a comfortable, quiet place to sit or lie down.

2. Close your eyes.

3. Give yourself permission to relax and let go of any outside stressors.

4. Slowly inhale through your nose, feeling the good air traveling all the way in. Allow the air to push down your diaphragm.

5. Pause for a count of four, and then exhale slowly through your mouth.

6. Say "one" to yourself.

7. Repeat steps 4 and 5. This time say "two" to yourself.

8. Repeat steps 4 and 5 until you have reached the number ten.

You might prefer starting with ten and working your way down to one.

You might want to say "relax" to yourself during the pause between inhaling and exhaling.

You can eventually shorten the number of breaths you take to three or four, so you can use this technique more quickly when needed in real-life situations.

More to Do

Practice relaxation. During full body relaxation, you quiet you muscles and nervous system. Even better, you quiet your mind. Here's how.

1. Start relaxing either from the tip of your toes upward or from the top of your head downward. Use your muscle groups for focus: feet and toes, calves and lower legs, thighs and upper legs, hips and pelvis, stomach muscles, chest area, back, shoulders and neck, jaw, face (especially eyes and temples), forehead, and top and back of head.

2. Remember to keep breathing deeply and slowly as you relax. Take as long as you like, but at least fifteen to twenty minutes, so you can really feel your body relaxing.

3. You might want to add a few calming thoughts to this exercise, such as *This feels good, I have all the time in the world,* or *I feel safe.*

4. If your brain insists on thinking worrisome thoughts like *I don't have time to do this* or *What should I make for dinner tonight?* or *This isn't working* or *I'm too busy to relax* or *I'm still mad at so-and-so,* just imagine these thoughts being tied to a balloon and drifting away. The idea is not to try to stop

having these thoughts but to let them depart because they aren't getting much attention.

5. You might want to add some visual, auditory, or tactile images to your relaxation exercise. For example, think of a time when you felt completely at peace with the world. For instance, you might recall a time when you were sitting on an ocean beach, feeling the sun warming you, listening to the waves and watching pelicans flying silently over the waves. Or perhaps you're thinking of a time when you were rocking in your favorite chair, eyes shut, glad to be alive, and happy with the universe. You can increase the power of your relaxation exercise by incorporating images like these, recalling certain images, sounds, or sensations.

Breathing well is the first way to stay calm or to quiet yourself when you've begun to get angry, but you can do even more when you combine your breathing exercise with full body relaxation.

8: ANGER INVITATIONS

What to Know

An *anger invitation* is our term for anything that happens (inside your mind and body or in the external world) that you could become angry about. Every day brings many invitations for anger: the driver who cuts you off without warning, waking up with a stomachache, someone carelessly leaving their cell phone on so it rings at the wrong time, your partner asking you to buy groceries on the way home when you've already had a long day, forgetting someone's name, a problem at work with the forklift or copying machine, and so on.

The trick is to be able to say "No thanks" to most of these invitations to get angry. If you don't learn that trick, you'll be getting angry many times every day. True, you'll always have a reason for your anger. But think of the time, energy, and effort you'll be wasting. You need to become very selective in accepting anger invitations.

How many invitations do you think you've received in the last twenty-four hours? How many have you accepted? Are there any differences between the ones you've accepted and the ones you've declined? Here's the big question: How many anger invitations do you think you'll accept in the next twenty-four hours?

Many anger invitations come from the people in your life. Picture them casting out a fishing line with these anger invitations as bait. Imagine them dangling this bait while trolling down the river of your emotions.

You are the fish. Hopefully, you are a fish that doesn't want to snatch the anger bait. You need to be a smart fish. Be very choosy about what you eat. Swim quietly in the weeds where you are hard to locate. Above all, remember this saying: *smart fish don't bite.*

What to Do

Be a smart fish. "Smart fish don't bite" means practicing these things:

Learn to react to others less aggressively: laugh things off; don't let little things bother you.

Don't waste your energy trying to make the river flow your way: go with the flow.

Choose your battles carefully: remember, the fish that bites loses most of the time.

Learn how and when others are trying to hook you: don't give them the fun of reeling you in.

Stay in control of your choices: get angry when something is worth fighting for, not just because someone threw a line into the water.

Think of three times recently when you got hooked. What happened? Will you remember that smart fish don't bite the next time these situations arise?

9: DEFUSE A POTENTIAL CONFLICT

What to Know

Okay, you start getting angry. But you can stop yourself if you just keep your head. Here are thirty-nine ways to keep a disagreement from escalating into a fight. It's up to you to utilize them. To do so, you'll need to recognize the signs that you are starting to become angry and any indicators that you and the person with whom you are talking are getting into dangerous territory. If either of you is starting to get loud, repeating your statements, becoming physically agitated, talking without listening, blaming or shaming the other person, and so on, get out your list of thirty-nine ways to defuse a potential conflict, and select one to use.

1. Just walk away.

2. Apologize.

3. Take three deep breaths.

4. Look for a compromise.

5. Tell yourself this is no big deal (not a crisis).

6. Sit down.

7. Talk softly and slowly.

8. Give a compliment.

9. Acknowledge the other's view ("You have a point there…").

10. Make a joke to lighten the mood.

11. Remind yourself that smart fish don't bite (you can say no to anger invitations).

12. Step back a little.

13. Stop drinking.

14. Give gentle touch.

15. Put yourself in the other person's shoes.

16. Take a time-out (remember the four Rs: recognize, retreat, relax, return).

17. Commit to being loving instead of warring (don't treat the people you care about like enemies).

18. Think of something you like about the other person.

19. Make a small concession ("All right, I'll do that the way you want me to.").

20. Argue the other person's side (to gain understanding).

21. Tell yourself to cool down—and then cool down.

22. Let the other person have the last word.

23. Focus on solutions, not victories or defeats.

24. Do something different, to break the escalation pattern.

25. Remind yourself to stay in control.

26. Stay in the present.

27. Keep your mouth shut instead of hurling insults.

28. Think in *both/and* terms instead of *either/or.*

29. Ask yourself what a calm friend would do in this situation.

30. Don't take things too personally.

31. Take the other person's concerns seriously.

32. Think, *I'm okay; you're okay.*

33. Act as if you were calm—and pretty soon you will be.

34. Treat your hot thoughts like clouds in the sky that will soon disappear.

35. Remember what could happen if you say or do something stupid.

36. Make yourself really listen.

37. Do something nice (like bringing the other person a cup of coffee).

38. Respond to an attack with caring and compassion.

39. If this is your partner or child, remember that you love them.

What to Do

Go through the list. Select five or six techniques that you believe would be most helpful when you have a disagreement with your partner, friend, parent, coworker, or whomever you are thinking about right now. Don't select only the ones you are most familiar with, though. Choose one or two techniques that would be new for you. You might pick "Respond to an attack with caring and compassion" if normally you are a very competitive individual who would be inclined to respond to an attack with a counterattack. Or perhaps you could try "Think of something you like about the other person" if you would usually do just the opposite during a dispute.

Write down these five or six techniques on a small card that you can carry with you. Look at the card at least twice a day. Then, when it's crunch time, at the beginning of a disagreement, you'll be able to review the list in your mind and choose one technique to use.

Are you familiar with the saying "If you only have a hammer in your toolkit, then every problem becomes a nail"? There are no miracle techniques that work every time with anger, and you need to have many tools at your disposal. Use the five or six you've selected to find out which ones work best with different people and for you. And don't hesitate to return to the list and select other techniques to try out as you master or reject the first five or six.

More to Do

Here's the ultimate challenge for you: Look through the list once again. Locate the three techniques that you think would be hardest to pull off. Ask yourself why that would be. For example, perhaps "Stay in the present" would be very difficult for you because you're so good at bringing up the past during a disagreement. Put one of these three techniques on your short list and commit to trying it out soon. You might discover you are more flexible than you thought as well as better at handling your anger.

10: TWENTY-FOUR-HOUR COMMITMENT TO ACT CALM

What to Know

You're reading this book because you want to change. Chances are you've been struggling with anger for a long time, and you don't like how it affects you and those you love. Looking back, you can remember plenty of situations where you said or did things out of anger that you later wished deeply you could undo. And you've probably resolved—many times—to speak more calmly or gently, to be more understanding and less blaming, or simply to keep the lid on.

It hasn't worked. You remembered for a few hours or a few days. Then something pushed your buttons and, before you knew it, all your best intentions were swept away. You may have felt guilty and bad—disgusted with yourself that your reactions seemed so automatic, so difficult to control. Perhaps you have felt helpless, watching yet another wave of anger sweep over you. It wells up in your stomach, flooding you with the need to shout and blame.

For some people, anger feels more like a cold rage, deep and poisonous. It leaks out a little at a time but never resolves, never heals. Something is terribly wrong or unfair; you feel trapped and in pain. Nothing you do seems to make the anger better, so it sets up housekeeping in your gut.

Effective anger management starts with a specific, time-limited decision, so make a commitment to act calm for twenty-four hours. Notice it is not a commitment to *be* calm; it's a commitment to *act* calm. You need to commit to yourself and to key people in your life that you are going to behave in a calm, nonaggressive way. Not forever. That's impossible; no one could promise such a thing. Not even for a week. That's far too long, given how strong and habitual your anger response is. Your commitment is just for a single twenty-four-hour day.

What to Do

Here's how to get started:

1. Tell people. Share with every significant person in your life that you are absolutely committed to behaving in a calm way between X and X. Explain that this means you won't shout at, swear at, hit, blame, attack, or denigrate *anyone*. Absolutely. No exceptions or excuses. Let them know that you're going to be vigilant and on guard for aggressive behavior throughout the designated time period.

2. Ask for help. There's a good chance—especially if you experience frequent, unpredictable anger—that this won't be easy. So you need real help, not just people's good wishes. Give family and friends a nonverbal signal they can use to let you know if you're looking or sounding angry. Something like a referee's time-out sign, or the gesture an umpire uses when a player slides in safe, or just a slowly descending hand that means "relax, calm down." Whatever signal you want to use, write it down and tell people how it works.

3. Prepare yourself in advance so that whenever you see the signal you will stop whatever you are doing until you can once again appear calm. Remember, you don't have to be calm; you just have to act calm.

4. See the benefit. What's the number one thing you want to achieve through anger management? A better relationship with your spouse, your kids, your friends? A chance to heal old wounds with your family? A better shot at rewards and promotions at work? A renewed feeling of pride and self-worth? An end to dangerous or costly behavior? Whatever is your biggest and best reason for acting calm, write it down and refer back to it when you need a reminder.

Once the twenty-four hours is up, check in with yourself. How did it go?

PART 2

UNDERSTANDING YOUR ANGER

When it comes to managing anger, the first step is actually to understand your anger. This may seem counterintuitive. You may think the best way to manage your anger is to avoid it whenever possible—to try to not be in touch with your anger—so you aren't at risk of acting on it. But trying to manage your anger by avoiding it is a lot like trying to find your way around a new city without a map. If you have no idea how the streets are laid out, getting from one place to another without getting lost is very difficult.

The same is true for your anger. It's going to be a lot more difficult to navigate your anger if you don't know all of its nooks and crannies and twists and turns. Therefore, an important step in managing your anger is to get in touch with it and understand all aspects of it. This includes understanding the types of situations and experiences that tend to bring up anger for you—or the cues for your anger—as well as understanding your own personal experience of anger.

11: YOUR ANGER CUES

What to Know

Although there are probably times when it feels like your anger comes out of the blue, all emotions are cued, or triggered, by something. That's the way emotions work. Even if you aren't able to figure out what cued your anger in any given moment, rest assured that something did. And knowing what tends to cue your anger will make you better prepared to manage it.

When identifying the cues for your anger, it's important to describe them in a particular way. The dialectical behavior therapy (DBT) skill of objectively labeling your experience (Linehan 1993b, 2015) allows you to describe these cues in a neutral, matter-of-fact way by just sticking to the facts. Rather than judging or evaluating the situations or experiences that bring up anger for you—which would probably only add fuel to the fire and make you angrier—you simply describe these experiences exactly as they are.

For example, let's say that your father said something that angered you. Describing the situation objectively would mean describing exactly what happened and what he said. Instead of saying "He was rude" or "He was a jerk," you'd say, "My dad called me this morning and told me that he doesn't approve of my job and thinks I should do something else." Separate your evaluations ("rude") and judgments ("jerk") from the facts (what your father actually said and did). Objectively labeling your experience will not only help you identify the specific cues for your anger, so you can address them head-on, but also keep you from adding fuel to the fire and fanning the flames of your anger.

You may notice that evaluations and judgments continue to pop into your head from time to time, especially when you first start practicing this skill. This is natural and to be expected. If this happens, simply notice the evaluation or judgment and bring your attention back to describing the experience objectively. The goal is not to get rid of judgments and evaluations completely, which would be impossible, but to avoid getting caught up in them as much.

Many types of experiences and situations can elicit feelings of anger. Although some of the most common cues for anger involve someone or something threatening your well-being (or the well-being of someone you care about) or blocking you from something you want, these cues can take a number of different forms. Therefore, it's important to figure out what brings up anger for you.

What to Do

Close your eyes and take a few minutes to think about times you experienced anger recently and what was going on then. Ask yourself if certain types of situations and experiences tend to bring up anger for you. Situations, events, people, or objects can be anger cues.

The following list contains common cues for anger. Consider if any apply to you:

Waiting in line

Not getting what you want

Having someone disagree with you

Being cut off while driving

Being told no

Driving in traffic

Being insulted

Being attacked

Chronic pain

Being prevented from doing something you want to do

Not having your opinions or wishes taken into account

Calling customer service

Being overcharged

Observing people mistreating animals, children, or other adults

Are there other situations that tend to bring up feelings of anger? If so, write them down in your journal.

More to Know

One of the things that can make anger so overwhelming is the sense that it comes out of the blue, and knowing the types of situations and experiences that tend to bring up feelings of anger is an important first step in learning to manage your anger. Anything that's unpredictable, whether it's an emotion, a thought, or a stressful situation, tends to be a lot more difficult to manage than something we can predict. Therefore, the better you become at pinpointing the situations and experiences that bring up anger for you, the more manageable your anger will be. Becoming more aware of your personal anger cues will also allow you to plan ahead and use some of the other skills in this book.

12: PHYSICAL SENSATIONS THAT GO ALONG WITH ANGER

What to Know

Most people experience an increase in energy and agitation when they are angry, because anger is an energizing emotion. The physical sensations that tend to go along with anger involve arousal and activation. What's interesting about these sensations is that they might be telling you that your body is preparing for action. Anger is one part of your body's natural defense system, often referred to as the *fight-or-flight response*. A lot of the physical sensations that go along with anger or fear involve changes in blood flow, which enable us to use our arms and legs more effectively to either defend ourselves or flee. Changes in blood flow can cause increased heart rate, perspiration, narrowing of vision (in order to focus attention on a threat), muscle tension, increased sensitivity in hearing, racing thoughts, increased respiration, and dry mouth.

Getting away from the danger (flight) is a common behavioral response to fear. With anger, however, a common reaction is to fight—move toward, through, or around—whatever is in your way. This reaction is why anger often goes hand in hand with the desire to act aggressively.

If you get used to noticing the physical signs of anger, you're one step closer to being able to identify and manage it more effectively. If you can identify bodily signs of anger before the signs get really intense, you can take action to avoid doing or saying things you may later regret.

What to Do

Here are some physical sensations commonly associated with anger. Identify any that apply to you:

Increased perspiration

Increased heart rate

Pounding heart

Increased respiration

Tense muscles

Clenching or tightening in the chest

Tightness in the jaw

Dry mouth

Tunnel vision

Feeling like things are not real

Flushing of the face

Feeling like you're going to explode

Activation of fight-or-flight response

Do you experience other physical sensations not listed? If so, write them down in your journal.

Practice paying attention to small changes that occur in your body when you begin to feel angry. Noticing physical sensations of anger early makes it easier to regulate and control your reactions.

13: THOUGHTS THAT GO ALONG WITH ANGER

What to Know

Sometimes angry thoughts can set off your anger. How you think about or interpret a situation can influence how angry you feel: very angry, mildly annoyed, or not angry at all. For example, many people feel anger when they don't get what they asked for. Even though anger is a common reaction to being told no, it's not the only reaction people can have. It all comes down to how you interpret the situation. If you believe that you deserve what you're asking for and have a right to get it, you're probably going to feel anger if someone says no to a request you make. On the other hand, if you don't believe that you deserve what you asked for, or you think it was a selfish or silly request, you might feel guilty or embarrassed if someone says no. The bottom line is that our interpretation of a situation is often just as important to the emotion we experience as the situation itself.

The thoughts that often go along with anger tend to focus on people, things, or situations being unfair, unjust, wrong, or simply not as they *should* be. In fact, the presence of the words "should" or "unfair" in your mind are excellent clues that you may be experiencing an anger-related thought. So the next time you find yourself thinking that something shouldn't have happened, or that things should be different, or that someone should be doing something else, or that things aren't fair, take a step back and consider whether or not you are feeling anger.

Thoughts of *should* and *unfair* are not the only thoughts that go along with anger. Furthermore, the thoughts that go along with anger for you may be different from the thoughts that accompany anger for someone else. To learn more about your own personal experience of anger, it's important to figure out the specific thoughts that tend to accompany feelings of anger for you.

What to Do

When you experience anger, do you find yourself thinking certain words or phrases or having certain thoughts? Consider if any of these thoughts and interpretations accompany anger for you:

This shouldn't have happened.

This isn't fair.

This isn't right.

That person shouldn't have done that.

What a jerk!

I hate…

This is so unfair.

They should be doing…

This person or situation is wrong.

Everyone is against me.

Are there other thoughts that often go through your mind when you're angry? Write them down in your journal, so you can notice these thoughts when they come up again. Catching anger early on—before it becomes incredibly intense—will make it easier to regulate.

14: ACTIONS THAT GO ALONG WITH ANGER

What to Know

The actions, or behavioral component, of your emotions may actually be the first thing you notice as you work on increasing your awareness of anger. Even before you notice the thoughts going through your mind or your physical sensations, you may become aware of your urges to do something or to act in a certain way. In fact, there might even be times when you don't realize you're feeling angry until you've acted on your anger in some way, for example, by yelling at a friend or punching a wall.

So, when you experience anger, what do you want to do? Do you have an urge to respond in a certain way? Do you want to scream or throw or hit something? Becoming more aware of your urge to take action will help you stop and reconsider before you do something that you may later regret.

What to Do

What types of things do you want to say or do when you feel anger? Consider whether any of these action urges associated with anger apply to you:

Pick a fight.

Raise your voice.

Scream.

Throw something.

Punch or hit something.

Stand up for yourself.

Assert your needs.

Destroy something.

Protect someone.

Hurt yourself.

Confront someone.

Voice your opinion.

Write down those urges that apply to you. If you have other action urges with anger, write them down as well.

Next, think about the things you actually do when you feel anger. Make sure you consider everything you tend to do, both positive and negative. Identifying the healthy ways you express anger is just as important as identifying the ways you express anger that don't work as well. Doing so can highlight the strengths and skills you already have, as well as those areas you may need to work on. Do you take any of these actions associated with anger?

Pick a fight.

Raise your voice.

Scream.

Throw something.

Punch or hit something.

Stand up for yourself.

Assert your needs.

Protect someone.

Hurt yourself.

Confront someone.

Voice your opinion.

Destroy something.

Take action.

Threaten others.

Criticize others.

Stand up for someone else.

Beat yourself up.

Complain.

Write down those actions that apply to you, and write down anything else you tend to do when you feel anger.

Take a moment to reflect on what you've learned here. Do you tend to act on all of your action urges, or do you act on some and not on others? For example, you may have an urge to raise your voice and yell when you feel anger, and find that this is something you do a lot when you're angry. On the other hand, you may have other urges, such as to punch someone or destroy something, that you've never acted on.

15: THE SHORT FUSE PROBLEM

What to Know

The anger problem that most frequently gets people into trouble is having a short fuse. Something disturbing takes place and—boom!—you go off like a firecracker. You explode. This problem is also called having a "hair-trigger temper," when almost anything can upset you, including many things that most everyone else simply ignores.

What are your most common triggers? Your kids arguing at the breakfast table? Someone cutting you off as you drive to work? A coworker's "stupid" remark? A little glitch on a project that keeps you from doing exactly what you want exactly when you want? A small, maybe unintended, criticism your partner makes during dinner? Not being able to find the television remote control? A nighttime call from a telephone solicitor? Trying to come up with a way to pay your bills when money is tight? Getting grumpy and irritable because you are sleep deprived?

How often do you become angry? Once an hour, twice a day, every morning, late at night?

What to Do

Carry a small notepad and a pencil with you for a week. Start a fresh page every morning. Keep your notepad with you at all times. Then every time you get angry—even just a little angry—make a mark in that notebook. If you have time, you might want to add some information about what was going on that triggered your anger. But that's not absolutely necessary. What's most important is for you to tally up how often you let yourself become angry every day.

More to Do

You can also measure how frequently you say and do positive things that prevent or cut off your anger. For example, you might make a check mark (or a longer entry) in your notebook each time you give praise to someone in your family. Take note of every time-out you take that helps prevent a nasty argument. Write down each time you practice breathing more deeply or do a relaxation exercise that helps you stay calm. It's also a good idea to write down in your notepad or a journal the thoughts you use to stay calm in anger-provoking situations. These positive choices will help you both stay in control of your anger and replace negative, anger-increasing thoughts and behaviors with positive, anger-reducing ones.

Here's a warning, though. Don't expect your hair-trigger temper to entirely go away. Chances are that your anger comes on too fast and too strong for you to prevent it from ever occurring. Someone says something negative to you (or at least you think it is negative) and—boom!—here comes that familiar adrenaline rush. Your muscles start to tense up. You feel a sudden impulse to attack.

But now comes the critical point. Just because you've got an adrenaline rush doesn't mean you must act on it. You don't have to blow up. Instead, allow the adrenaline to course through your veins. Notice the feeling. Observe it from a little distance, almost as if it were happening to someone else. It will probably only take half a minute or so for the adrenaline surge to begin dissipating. Pretty soon it will be gone. Sure, you'll miss an opportunity to let someone have it for whatever they said or did. But who cares? What's really important is that you gained mastery over the impulse to attack. And that's exactly what anger management is all about.

16: MANAGING INTENSITY BY RATING YOUR ANGER

What to Know

Anger is an emotion. It tells you that something is going wrong. It gives you the energy to take action. Anger can help you reach your goals. But it is important to keep your anger in proper perspective. Otherwise you'll find yourself getting really upset over trivial insults. Then you'll overreact. It can help to gain awareness by rating your anger. Here are some ways to do that.

What to Do

How strongly would you rate your anger right now, on a scale of 0 to 10, where 0 is "I'm not angry at all," 5 is "I'm fairly mad but still well in control," and 10 is "I'm so furious I'm completely out of control"?

People with anger problems consistently rate their anger as a 7, 8, 9, or 10. It's as if they seldom experience just a little anger. Instead, they tend to become highly angry over even apparently little offenses.

So here is another question: On a scale of 0 to 10, how serious is the problem that is triggering your anger? Is it big or small or somewhere in between?

Do you see where this is going? You have a significant anger problem if you consistently rate your anger high when the problem is small.

The *heat index* is another way to rate your anger. When people talk about their anger, they often use a lot of temperature analogies: "I was boiling hot." "I kept my cool." "I was hotter than a pistol." "I stayed cool as a cucumber." "I was steaming mad." "I was hot under the collar."

These heat references make a lot of sense. Your body does heat up when you're angry, because anger is a response to a perceived threat or danger. Your natural fight-or-flight response calls on your body to provide energy to make your legs run, your arms strong, and your whole system ready for action. It's natural to feel hot when bothered.

If the numeric scale of 0 to 10 doesn't mean much to you when rating your anger, try this instead: ask yourself how hot you're getting about the situation. And while you're at it, you might want to ask yourself if you need to cool down a little before you say or do anything.

You may want to design your own personal *anger thermometer* to help you decide just how angry you are in any situation. Use your own words to describe how hot you are at any given moment. Your thermometer might look like this:

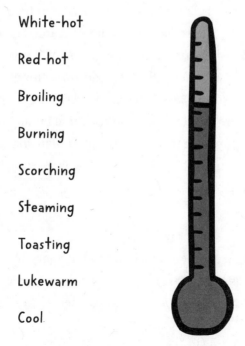

White-hot

Red-hot

Broiling

Burning

Scorching

Steaming

Toasting

Lukewarm

Cool

Your Anger Thermometer

17: REACTING TOO QUICKLY OR STRONGLY

What to Know

"I wish I could keep my mouth shut for a couple minutes when I get mad," says Nina. "I often regret the first words I speak." Nina's problem is that she hasn't learned to cut off her immediate negative reaction to something that annoys her. She instantaneously goes from feeling attacked or insulted to counterattacking. Nina seems to lack an inner voice that would tell her to slow down and think about the situation before she does anything.

"My wife hates it when I swear a blue streak or throw things around," says Jesse. "She says I overreact. But I get so angry I have to do something. Besides, isn't it bad for your health to hold your anger in?" It's as if Jesse only has an on/off switch rather than a more sophisticated regulator in his brain. When he gets mad, he gets intensely mad. And then he overreacts. He says and does things way out of proportion to the problem he's facing. Furthermore, he justifies his anger in two ways: first by convincing himself that he simply must lose his cool and then by arguing that he needs to ventilate his anger for his health.

What to Do

Are you like Nina? If so, then remember to tell yourself to *Always buy time*. In other words, when you're angry, take some time before you act. Repeat the phrase *Always buy time* to yourself several times a day for at least a week.

If you're like Jesse, remember to tell yourself to *Stay in control.* You must take full responsibility for your actions. Swearing a blue streak is a choice, not a necessity. Repeat the phrase *Stay in control* to yourself several times a day for at least a week.

More to Know

These two problems—getting angry too quickly and reacting too strongly to anger—often occur when you react to an irritating situation as if it were a threatening one. Your brain is basically misinterpreting the problem and making it a much bigger deal than necessary. It needs to be calmed.

There are two pathways in the brain that handle possibly threatening stimuli. The first is the fast path. Here messages are transported from the hypothalamus directly to the amygdala. The result is immediate action. This pathway is very important if and when you are faced with an immediately dangerous situation—for instance, if you are threatened by a bully on the street.

There is an alternative pathway, though, a slower path that takes longer because it goes through the newer parts of the brain, allowing for higher-level processing. The result is a more measured response. While the fast path works best for immediate danger, such as a truck barreling toward you, the slower path works better for less threatening dangers, including the kind of personal annoyances common in day-to-day living.

You may not be able to keep from having a fast-path reaction, since it happens so quickly and is mostly out of your conscious control. Nevertheless, your job with regard to anger control is to make every effort to choose to take the slow path. You are buying time to think out better responses to situations that trigger your anger. Taking a time-out is the single-best way to reduce your risk of an immediate overreaction.

More to Do

Here's something else to try. Every time you start to get mad, tell yourself, *Hey, my brain is getting this all wrong. I'm not in danger. I don't need to panic. I don't need to overreact. I need to take my time before I say or do anything.* The idea is to very intentionally intercept your brain's overreaction. You can essentially redirect your brain to travel on the slow path instead of the fast path.

Now this is no easy job. Once the messages start moving on the fast path, your body immediately gets ready for a fight. You will have to be firm with your own brain. Treat it like a kid who needs to be guided onto the correct road. Get that kid off the freeway and onto the side streets. Remember that every time you do this, your brain will get better at seeking out the slower pathway first. Gradually you'll need to spend less time redirecting it. Eventually your brain will get the idea and automatically steer itself onto the slower path whenever you begin to get upset.

18: GETTING TOO ANGRY TO LISTEN

What to Know

Anger is a messenger. It tells you that something is wrong in your life. Anger lets you know that you're in danger or that something is blocking your path. It suggests that you consider taking action to fight the threat or to unblock the path. Frequently anger tries giving you these messages by shouting at the top of its lungs: *Listen to me! Listen to me! Listen to me!*

Meanwhile, your partner, your friend, your coworker, your child, your sister or brother, a customer—even a complete stranger—is trying to talk with you about whatever you're upset about. They want to try to work with you, to reassure you that you're safe or to negotiate with you about how to remove whatever obstacle is blocking the path. Too bad you can't hear them. It's as if you are wearing headphones with music blasting in your ears while they're trying to talk to you. Anger is taking up all your mental space.

You've got to take the headphones off. That means turning your anger off or at least turning down the volume enough so you can actually hear what the other person is saying. Here's how.

What to Do

Take a minibreak to gain time. Go to the restroom. Step outside. Get a snack from the kitchen.

When you're alone, take a few deep breaths and try to relax.

Say to yourself, *Thank you, anger—I've got the message. Please don't shout anymore. I need to think.* Take a few deep breaths.

Return to your conversation, this time really attending to what the other person is saying.

More to Know

Sometimes minibreaks aren't enough. You'll simply not be able to calm yourself enough to have a reasonable conversation, no matter how badly you'd like to do so. In that case you will need to take a longer time-out. But why is it so hard to cool off once you've become angry?

Your inability to think well or have a productive conversation when you become quite angry is perfectly normal. Strong anger triggers primitive survival instincts. The goal becomes living through the moment, not negotiating a win-win solution. So your body goes into attack-or-flee mode. Your muscles tense. You become supervigilant. And up goes your blood pressure. Once your blood pressure rises too high, you simply will not be able to have a meaningful conversation. This is less about fight or flight than about *fight or think.*

Flooding is a good name for this problem. Think of your anger as a river in your mind. Every so often, that river rises above its banks and floods towns with names like "Logic," "Compromise," "Caring," and "Calmness."

Some people are slow to flood; their anger rivers flow slowly and quietly almost all the time. Others must deal with relatively wild rivers, the kind with powerful currents and dangerous rapids. Maybe the worst situation is to have an anger river that runs through a slot canyon. One minute you're peacefully walking through the deep but narrow canyon. The next second you're fighting for your life as a torrent of water surges through the only channel it's got.

How quickly do anger floods recede? That depends on your brain and body. Some people need only a couple minutes even after becoming quite irate. Others need twenty-four to forty-eight hours to calm down.

More to Do

The critical issue here is how long does it take you to stop flooding? Do you know the answer to that question? If not, measure your pulse rate the next time you get mad. If it's over one hundred beats per minute, take a time-out and try to relax. Keep measuring your pulse rate to see how long it takes before it drops back under one hundred. But notice that if you start thinking about what got you so mad, your pulse rate will probably quickly rise again.

19: BECOMING RESENTFUL

What to Know

Anger is supposed to be a brief signal that something is wrong. The message in anger is this: "Hey, something is blocking my path. I need to push it out of the way." The goal is for you to receive the signal, do something productive, and then let go of your anger.

But what if something goes wrong? For instance, you notice your teenager hasn't cleaned up her room for days. You get angry. You confront her and tell her to clean her room. Instead of obeying, she merely grunts and walks away. Three days later her room is still a mess. Now you're really mad. You repeat your requests. She ignores you again and again and again.

Slowly your anger builds to resentment. Resentment is extended anger. What should be a sprint has turned into a marathon.

What to Do

Later you'll learn some ways to deal with resentments, especially by using forgiveness. But for now, here are the main characteristics, so you can see if you are burdened by resentment. Are you familiar with these traits?

- You feel stuck with angry feelings and thoughts about someone; you can't get rid of those feelings and thoughts.

- You think mostly about the bad things someone has done while ignoring their positive qualities.

- Sometimes you believe that you actually hate the person you resent.

- You see the offender as a bad person instead of someone who has done things you don't like.

- The quality of your life suffers because you spend too much time thinking about someone you dislike.

If one or more of these statements applies to you, then your anger has turned into resentment.

More to Know

"Don't let someone have free rent in your brain." The speaker, Ed, was addressing his alcoholism at an open AA meeting many years ago. Ed had relapsed several times over the last decade; each time he went back to drinking, it was over a resentment that kept growing bigger and bigger over time. At first, he said, his anger was like a little pebble that kept rolling around in his mind, but that little pebble grew into a rock, a boulder, and finally a mountain. The larger his resentment became, the more time and energy it demanded. Eventually Ed found himself spending hours every day thinking about how various people—his ex-wife, a former employer, his estranged daughter—had so badly mistreated him. He began thinking of these people as totally evil. He said, "I became utterly consumed with my hatreds." He became overwhelmed as anger took over his brain and his body.

And then Ed relapsed. He drank in a desperate effort to forget his pain. But even that effort backfired. "I drank to forget. Instead, the more I drank, the angrier I became. So then I'd drink more to try to forget what my drinking mind was remembering." Fortunately, Ed ended his talk by celebrating the five years he'd stayed sober. His formula for success included taking time every morning and every evening to let go of his resentments and to be grateful for the good things in his life.

Ed's story provides two major lessons:

Hanging on to resentments can ruin your life. After you've let go of a resentment, you can see what a terrible waste of time and energy it was. Unfortunately, resentment never seems to be a waste of time and energy while you're holding on to it. Instead, you feel totally justified in your anger. *Just look at what that guy did to me,* you think. *How could I not keep thinking about him? How could I not want revenge? Why should I stop hating him?* Your resentment feels like a life raft in a sea of desperation. What you don't realize at the time is that the water isn't really all that deep. If you'd only let go of that raft, you could easily wade back to shore.

Developing a positive daily ritual can help you let go of resentments. Resentments tend to be sneaky and persistent, hanging around the edges of your soul, waiting for an opportunity to return. (It's not unlike addiction, which is why resentments are such a problem for recovering addicts.) However, a good routine or ritual can remind you that there are better things to think about. Ed developed a twice-daily routine that helped him remember each day to put his gratitude ahead of his resentments and his joy for life ahead of his anger at life.

Are you ready to let go of the life raft of resentment, so you can freely swim in the sea of life again? What kind of ritual or routine would help you alleviate your resentments?

20: KNOWING YOUR PAYOFFS

What to Know

It would be easy to quit being so angry if you were punished every time you blew a gasket. But reality is more complicated than that. You may be reluctant to give up your anger because you receive payoffs (rewards) by getting angry. Perhaps you don't get a payoff every time you get angry—but just often enough to keep you going. At any rate, it's important that you become fully aware of how your anger benefits you. Only then can you make an informed decision to give up receiving these payoffs so you can live a better life.

What to Do

Here are some common payoffs for getting or staying mad. Identify which of these payoffs most apply to you and your anger.

I get what I want when I get angry.

I push people away so I can have some space for myself.

Getting angry is my way of making others listen to me.

By becoming angry I force people to leave me alone.

I do things my way—my anger warns people not to tell me what to do.

I feel in control when I get angry.

I avoid other feelings, such as anxiety and sadness, by getting angry.

I gain power over others when I get angry.

I like it that people are afraid of me when I get angry.

I don't have to take responsibility for my actions when I get mad.

I use anger to hide feelings of shame, guilt, and low self-worth from myself and others.

I gain status with my anger—people treat me with greater respect.

I like the strong feelings I have when I get angry—I feel alive and energetic.

People pay more attention to me when I become angry.

Are there other payoffs you can think of? Write them down in your journal.

More to Do

Okay, so now you know your payoffs. But remember that your payoffs must be balanced against the costs of your anger. This is a good time for you to go back to chapter 2 to review the immediate and longer-term costs you've experienced because of your anger. Think again about the people you've driven away and the financial losses, mental anguish, and unnecessary pain that your anger has caused you. It's pretty likely that these penalties far exceed the rewards for your anger. Why else would you be reading this book?

So why, then, have you hung on to your anger so long when it costs you far more than it rewards you? Maybe it's the fact that the payoff comes first. You yell first and regret it later. Immediate gratification often wins out over long-term well-being. Just ask the cocaine addict or compulsive spender about that.

Of course, there is another possibility. Perhaps your anger has become such a deeply ingrained habit that you simply can't let it go. Becoming angry has become an automatic, unthinking way of reacting to the universe. Maybe you react to almost everything with anger even if that response makes no sense. Your anger has become your default option in life, the emotion that is always on until you learn how to turn it off. If so, the payoffs are only part of the picture. Once a habit develops, it can go on for decades even after it stops being rewarding. Now you get angry just because you get angry. Do you think your anger has become a habit? If so, are you willing to let it go?

PART 3

GETTING UNSTUCK FROM ANGER

Sometimes, no matter how hard you've worked on anger management skills, a provocative situation will get the best of you. It can be discouraging and costly, particularly if your temper pushes you into some seriously aggressive or destructive behavior.

Don't give up. If you look back over your progress, you'll probably see a lot of ups and downs. There were flare-ups and periods when you were coping more effectively. Some provocations were clearly harder than others. So if you're charting your progress, you will see a sawtooth profile. On average, though, if you've been using the tools offered in these chapters, you are likely to be angry less often and less intensely than you were at the start of this book.

That said, what can you do now if some provocation really gets to you? Or if a problem or conflict has become chronically upsetting? Let's move into some effective strategies to get unstuck from anger.

21: AVOIDING ANGER AS A PERMANENT CONDITION

What to Know

Anger, especially when it gets combined with anxiety, can take over your brain. You begin fretting about something that's bugging you and, like the vine in Jack and the Beanstalk, it grows right before your eyes. Your anger juts skyward at the speed of thought. It grows wider and wider, too, so pretty soon you can't see or think about anything else. Your anger fills up your universe. It becomes the only thing in your life that matters. Like a bulldog, your anger won't let go. Worse yet, the longer it goes on, the stronger it becomes, so your fretting turns into fuming. And that means you can no longer think of any good solutions to the problem—your emotions have trumped your thinking ability. You have become obsessed.

What to Do

Think of at least three brief thoughts that can help you remember not to obsess. Here are some examples:

This is a real problem, but it isn't about life and death.

It's time to think about something good in my life.

Let go and let God.

I won't let my anger run my life.

I won't let my anger ruin my life.

Write these thoughts down. Keep them in your wallet, pocket, or purse. Read them every morning or whenever you start getting angry.

22: DON'T LET ANGER DRIVE THE BUS

What to Know

Obsessive anger leads to chronic anger. Once you start obsessing about how people have harmed you or whatever else triggers your anger, it gradually takes over your life.

Think of your life as a long bus trip. You are the driver of the bus, but you're not all alone. You have some very interesting passengers. They are your emotions: anger, joy, sadness, fear, shame, guilt, loneliness, and so on. Once in a while you let each of them sit next to you as you drive, but you are in charge of the bus.

Then something strange happens. Your anger stands up, strides to the front, grabs you by the neck, and throws you out of the driver's seat. "I'm hijacking this bus," anger announces, and then orders you to take a seat in the back.

What next? You're in for a wild ride. Your anger will go fast and furious while aiming for every pothole in the road. "Whee, what fun!" anger shouts. But somehow you're not really enjoying the ride all that much.

Then anger stops the bus and glares at your other emotions. Anger tells them to get off the bus: "We don't need any other feelings—I can handle whatever comes up." And so anger does. When your friend waves hello, your anger practically runs her down because you remember a time when she said something mean to you. When you see a family member sitting by the road waiting for a ride, your anger drives on by without a second glance. "Let her walk. She means nothing to me," says your anger, because anger is incapable of empathy.

When anger is in the driver's seat, it dominates your thinking. It becomes so strong and tenacious that it's almost like you become your anger. "I Am My Anger and My Anger Is Me" becomes the theme song of your life.

What to Do

If anger has taken over your life, you need to act assertively. Stand up, walk to the front of the bus, and firmly order your anger to get out of the driver's seat. Tell anger that you're back in control. Don't kick anger off the bus, though. Remember that anger can be useful to you, as long as it only comes up to the front when needed and you remain in the driver's seat even when anger is present.

You have one more job, of course. You need to round up the rest of your emotions and invite them back on the bus. Ask yourself which emotion you need to have get back on the bus first. Why is this emotion important to have in your life?

23: IDENTIFY THE FEELINGS UNDERNEATH YOUR ANGER

What to Know

One function of anger is to cover up emotional pain. Anger tends to block awareness of feelings such as shame, fear, or hurt. It's like a great big boulder that obscures a lot of your emotional landscape.

If anger usually gets the upper hand when you're dealing with certain provocations, it often means that the anger is protecting you from some other feeling—a feeling you'd prefer not to face. Overcoming anger in this situation may necessitate identifying that underlying feeling and finding an alternative way to cope with it.

What to Do

Visualize a recent provocation when your anger got the upper hand. Close your eyes and form an image of the setting—colors, shapes, sounds, smells, and physical sensations such as heat or texture. Notice who's there and listen to what's being said. Also notice any trigger thoughts you may have. Take some time to really anchor yourself in the scene.

Then hit the rewind button and go back to the beginning, just as your anger was getting started. Then go even a little further back—before the trigger thoughts and the anger—to what you first felt. Notice your inner climate at that moment. Stay with it. Take a few deep breaths and try to capture the emotion.

Now look at the following list to see if any of these feelings were present before the anger hit:

Guilt—a sense of having done something wrong

Shame—a deep feeling of being unacceptable, flawed, or contemptible

Hurt—a feeling of being devalued or denigrated by others

Loss—a feeling that something you needed or counted on is gone or missing

Hunger/frustrated drive—an aching for something; a strong sense of incompleteness

Helplessness—the feeling that there's nothing you can do about your pain, that crucial elements of your life are beyond your control

Anxiety/fear—a dread of something that could happen; a sense of danger; a fear of certain things or situations

Feeling unworthy—a sense that you aren't good enough, that you are bad or wrong or without intrinsic value

Emptiness—a sense of numbness or hollowness

In your journal, write down any feelings you notice that underlie your anger.

24: THREE STRATEGIES TO COPE WITH PAINFUL FEELINGS

What to Know

If you've identified one of the emotions in chapter 23 as being present just before your anger surged during a recent provocation, chances are the anger was functioning as a breakwater to keep the feeling from overwhelming you. Now there is an important task ahead. You need to find an alternative way to cope with this feeling *besides anger*. Here are three basic strategies to manage painful emotions.

What to Do

Start by simply accepting and holding the feeling for a while. It won't last forever. A common delusion when we're in pain is that there will never be an end to it. If you think back to struggles with similar emotions, however, you know that even the hardest ones to bear are time limited—eventually they pass. So notice the wave of the feeling hit, crest, and gradually recede. Take some deep breaths. Imagine the pain is next to you, not *in you*, or see it from a distance. Give it a color and shape. Watch while it slowly, slowly shrinks in size.

The second strategy is to use coping thoughts. Begin by noticing the thoughts that trigger your feeling. What are you saying to yourself that intensifies the pain? Write these thoughts down. Here are some examples:

Complete disaster! Total betrayal! How could she do something like that?

If you really cared about me, you would have helped me with the housework, and then I wouldn't be so exhausted and irritable.

His behavior is so disgusting that our social life is becoming a complete nightmare.

Now *rewrite* the negative thoughts following these key rules:

Make the thoughts accurate rather than exaggerated.

Make the thoughts specific rather than general.

Use language that is not belittling or insulting but is kind.

Include balancing realities and alternative explanations (the positive part of the picture that you're leaving out).

Here are some examples:

It's only a setback. It's not worth getting all bent out of shape about it.

I can ask for help and make a plan to take care of myself in this situation.

He thought he was being funny. I don't like his jokes, but I'm not responsible for his actions.

The third strategy for coping with difficult feelings is to develop a plan to solve the problem. What can you change in your life, in your relationships, or in your behavior to diminish this painful feeling? If you stop the angry blaming, maybe there's something you can do to make things different. Begin by writing out a clearly stated goal. Now brainstorm some solutions. List as many as you can think of. Quantity is better than quality. You can evaluate them later.

To illustrate the value of problem solving for anger control, consider Ricardo's struggle to take time off from his interior design business. Ricardo is irritable and exhausted, and he wants to spend time with his mother in New Mexico. Problem is, he has a one-man office and he's afraid that taking time off may result in him alienating his clients or dropping the ball on important projects.

Ricardo started with the clear goal: "I want two weeks both to relax and spend time with my mother." While brainstorming solutions, he came up with fourteen ideas ranging from "carry blueprints with me and conduct business by email" to "send clients some French Chardonnay and tell them to chill for two weeks."

Ricardo then looked at his top three solutions and listed positive and negative consequences for each one. For example, "staying in touch with clients while visiting Mom" had both advantages (allowing him to "put out fires" at work and stay in touch with key clients) and disadvantages (interrupting his vacation, keeping him from ever really relaxing, the feeling of being cheated).

Ricardo finally settled on the following idea: "Take two week-long vacations separated by a brief catch-up period." He planned to make no calls while he was gone. Decision made, Ricardo immediately booked his tickets to New Mexico.

25: PUTTING YOURSELF IN SOMEONE ELSE'S SHOES

What to Know

Empathy is the ability to get outside your own worldview temporarily so you can see, feel, and understand the world from somebody else's perspective. The evidence is clear and convincing: people who can put themselves in another's shoes for a while are much less likely to get into useless arguments and unnecessary conflicts. You can definitely improve your empathy skills by taking the time on a regular basis to practice placing yourself in the mind and emotions of another.

You'll need to improve two skills to get good at empathy: being curious and being nonjudgmental.

What to Do

The next time you get stuck in an argument, try to put yourself in the other person's shoes. It will help to ask yourself these questions:

Am I being judgmental? If so, could I place my judgments on hold for a while?

What is most important to the other person? What are their main values?

What are they feeling right now?

Have I ever been in a similar situation that would help me understand their viewpoint?

More to Know

Becoming more empathic isn't just about learning how to be curious and ask questions ("What are you feeling?") or how to be less judgmental. It's deeper than that. The real goal is to better comprehend the other person's life story.

Each of us organizes the key events in our lives in a single, meaningful narrative, or life story. Everyone's life story is unique and based on how we interpret events. For example, Sofia and Mina had similar experiences in their teens. Both of them lost their mothers to cancer, suffered through their father's subsequent depression and bout with alcoholism, and had to work long hours during high school to buy their own clothes because of their father's disability. Although the histories of these two women would appear similar, you can discover, by asking them to tell their life stories, how different they actually are.

Sofia has put those events together by constructing a narrative in which her main goal in life is to care for others. She set aside her dreams to go to college. Instead, she married early and is raising a family. Taking care of her father made her put the needs of others before her own; as a result, her children's needs are the center of her life. She is often exhausted and sometimes wonders who she is, but if you were to ask Sofia what she learned from her upbringing, she would say that taking care of family means everything.

Meanwhile, Mina created an entirely different meaning from the same events. She considers herself a survivor, someone who is tough, strong, and capable of anything. She devoted herself to a career as a consultant, specializing in troubleshooting difficult corporate situations. The meaning she took from her childhood is that you can't count on anybody to be there for you. Yes, sometimes she feels lonely, but she's unwilling to risk the pain of losing yet another person she loves. Consequently, she relies upon herself.

You'll never hear Sofia's or Mina's life story unless you ask them to tell it. That's what empathy is about. When you listen to another's life story with curiosity and without judgment, you are mastering the art of empathy.

More to Do

Ask a couple of people to tell you their life stories. If they ask you what you mean, tell them you'd like to hear about a few of the important events in their lives that helped make them who they are today.

26: DEEP BREATHING

What to Know

Deep breathing is a research-supported CBT method that can calm the mind and body by activating the parasympathetic nervous system, the part of the nervous system related to relaxation, positive moods, and less stress (Perciavalle et al. 2017). The relaxed state prompted by deep breathing is also associated with improved decision making (De Couck et al. 2019).

Deep breathing doesn't solve problems, but the process sets the stage for clear thinking and can serve as a distancing technique when anger starts to arise.

What to Do

Find a comfortable place where you have no distractions and where you can sit comfortably. Close your eyes. Loosen up by rolling your shoulders around from front to back and then from back to front.

1. Take in a full deep breath for a count of four (four seconds) until your belly expands.

2. Hold your breath for another count of four.

3. Exhale slowly to a count of four.

Repeat this three-part breathing exercise for three minutes. Do this twice a day at about the same time for two weeks. If this has a calming effect, continue.

There is nothing magical about three minutes. Some go for two minutes, others for ten. It depends on you.

If you feel angry just before doing a deep-breathing exercise, you may not experience an immediate effect. It takes time for your stress hormones to return to normal levels. Meanwhile, put yourself through the paces of a three-minute deep-breathing cycle. Wait twenty minutes. Go through the deep-breathing cycle again. See if that makes a difference in your anger.

27: PROGRESSIVE MUSCLE RELAXATION

What to Know

Learning to relax is an essential element in anger management. Remember, getting angry is a two-step process. First, physical tension or stress has to exist in the body; second, anger-triggering thoughts complete the picture. Half the anger battle can be won by simply learning to relax the physical tension that develops in provocative situations. It's a proven fact that if you can relax your body and keep it relaxed, it's almost impossible to get angry.

Combating stress using the skills you're about to learn can help you calm down, think clearly, and handle any situation in an effective, positive way. The eventual goal is to become so good at relaxing that you can let go of tension anytime, anywhere, in thirty seconds or less.

People usually do progressive muscle relaxation in a comfortable, distraction-free place on an easy chair or lying on a couch. Here's how. In an organized sequence, you tighten (without straining) and relax one major muscle group at a time. It helps to take about four seconds to tighten and four seconds to relax the tension in each of the muscle groups.

You can follow muscle relaxation with the deep-breathing exercise you learned in chapter 26, for an added effect. (*Caveat:* Do not tense areas of physical pain, injury, or recent surgery. And remove contact lenses.)

What to Do

Find a comfortable spot to practice either sitting or lying down. The process will take about three and a half minutes. There is no one right order for contracting and relaxing muscle groups. You can start with your face and work down toward your toes, reverse this sequence, or create another sequence. The important thing is to follow a routine pattern. The more relaxing effects come from tensing and relaxing facial and neck muscles. This sequence starts with the face.

Wrinkle your forehead. Let your forehead muscles relax.

Make a grinning face like the Cheshire cat. Let your cheek muscles relax.

Frown by tightening your lips downward. Let your lip muscles go limp.

Tighten your jaw. Let your jaw muscles relax.

Close your eyes until they are tight. Let your eyelids relax.

Press your tongue against the roof of your mouth. Let your tongue relax.

Pull your head gently forward until your chin touches your chest. Let your neck muscles relax.

Move your head back. Let your neck muscles relax.

Move your head to the right. Let your neck muscles relax.

Move your head to the left. Let your neck muscles relax.

Tighten your hands into fists. Let your hand muscles relax.

Turn your wrists down and tighten your forearms. Let your wrists and forearms relax.

Tighten your biceps. Let your biceps relax.

Stretch out your arms to tighten your triceps. Let your triceps relax.

Shrug your shoulders to tighten them. Let your shoulder muscles relax.

Pull your shoulders back. Let your shoulder muscles relax.

Pull your shoulders forward. Let your shoulder muscles relax.

Arch your back to make it feel tense. Let your back muscles relax.

Tighten your chest muscles. Let your chest muscles relax.

Push your stomach out so it looks like a potbelly. Let your stomach muscles relax.

Pull your stomach inward. Let your stomach muscles relax.

Tighten your buttocks. Let your buttock muscles relax.

Tighten your thighs. Let your thigh muscles relax.

Tighten your calf muscles by pointing your toes forward. Let your calf muscles relax.

Tighten your shin muscles by pointing your toes up. Let your shin muscles relax.

Now mentally go back over the entire procedure, and feel the relaxation in your feet, ankles, calves, back, and chest. Do some deep breathing. As you let go, more and more, the relaxation deepens in your neck, shoulders, arms, and hands. Go deeper and deeper into being relaxed. Finally, feel the relaxation extend to your head and face, your jaw hanging loose and your lips slightly parted.

If some tension persists in a specific part of your body, simply return your focus to that spot. Increase the tension, hold it, take a deep breath, and then relax. And let go.

28: USING I-STATEMENTS

What to Know

The purpose of an *I-statement* is to clearly tell someone exactly what bothers you and how you feel. It can be helpful in managing anger because it offers a solution that doesn't place blame on others but redirects the focus to how you're feeling about the situation. There are three parts to I-statements:

1. State what the other person has said or done that bothers you in specific terms, using facts when possible: "Yesterday you promised to talk with me this morning about our financial situation, but you slept in instead."

2. Tell the other person what you are feeling as a result of their actions: "I'm feeling angry and hurt. Plus I'm worried because we really do need to figure out how to pay the bills."

3. Now say exactly what you want to address how you're feeling: "I would feel better if you could sit down with me now so we can decide what to do about paying our bills."

What to Do

Think of a situation in your life right now in which you could use an I-statement. Now decide what statements you could use for each of the three parts. If it's helpful, write them down in your journal.

More to Know

I-statements look easy. But be wary of making these mistakes:

Being vague about what's bothering you, how you feel, or what you want: It's useless to say something like this: "Mateo, you're kinda mean to me, and I sorta feel bad, and I want you to be nicer." You need to give Mateo much more specific information about what he says that sounds mean, what you mean when you say you feel bad, and how he could say nicer things to you.

Saying "You make me feel...": Your feelings are your responsibility, not the other person's. Instead, reframe your statement using "I." "I feel..."

Name-calling or being insulting: Mateo probably won't respond to your I-statement very positively if you begin with "Mateo, you lazy worm..."

Expecting miracles: Just because you're using clear language doesn't guarantee you'll get what you want. But you can try.

Turning I-statements into a personality attack: Personality attacks are negative statements about some general characteristic of another individual. They often take the form of a *you-statement*: "You are so lazy." "You're a jerk." "You're stupid." These attacks can also masquerade as an I-statement: "I feel like you're being lazy." Saying this might make you feel better for a minute because hurting someone you're mad at can be satisfying. However, these kinds of assaults almost certainly will increase ill will. Besides, they are virtually useless in terms of actually getting someone to alter their behavior. Who would voluntarily change because someone is calling them names? Most people will do more of the same, not less, when insulted.

More to Do

Take responsibility for your own feelings, thoughts, and actions. You may think, *If only that person would quit being a jerk, then everything would be fine.* But what about you? Are you doing things that make the situation worse? Blaming the other party won't make things better, whereas determining how you can change the way you respond to them may.

Use I-statements to give positive feedback. That is, don't reserve them only for when something is bothering you. Why limit this powerful technique to negative situations? Why not reward others for positive behavior? It builds good will and good feelings toward others. Here is an example.

1. "Sally, yesterday you offered to take the kids to the zoo even though you had worked hard all day."

2. "I feel great when you take time with them. It warms my heart when I see them playing with you."

3. "Next time you go to the zoo, I'd like to go with you and the kids just to watch you having a good time together."

Everybody needs praise. I-statements allow you to fine-tune your praise so others learn exactly what they are doing that you like. When you give praise, be sure to avoid following it up with "but." Taking the previous example, don't add "…but you don't do enough with the kids most of the time." Now you've turned praise into criticism. Criticizing the other person will make them defensive, especially when it comes as a surprise attack.

29: FAIR-FIGHTING GUIDELINES

What to Know

All people disagree from time to time. That means a certain amount of conflict is inevitable. However, you can greatly affect the likelihood that your conflict will eventually have a positive result if you fight fair. A positive result occurs when the issue is resolved, at least for a while, and no one's feelings are hurt during the discussion.

Here is a list of the things you should avoid doing during a disagreement. Take a good look at these fair-fighting *don'ts* and decide which negative behaviors you need to stop.

Don't make fun of others: *"You're so cute when you get mad."*

Don't run away from the issue: *"I don't want to talk about it."*

Don't overgeneralize: *"You are always late."*

Don't be dismissive: *"Whatever!"*

Don't insist on getting in the last word: *"I've got to say one more thing…"*

Don't get stuck in the past: *"I'll never forget what you said last year."*

Don't hit, push, shove, or threaten: *"If you say that again, I'm gonna…"*

Don't stand up and yell or swear: *"@#^$%#!!"*

Don't interrupt: *"I'm going to jump in here."*

Don't make faces: *"What do you mean I made a face? I can't help it if I rolled my eyes."*

Don't make personal attacks: *"You're a loser and a horrible person."*

What to Do

You need to do more than just refrain from negative communication patterns. You'll need to develop some positive communication skills to use during disagreements if you really want to solve your conflicts rather than have them go on and on. Try these fair-fighting *dos* during conflict.

Stick to one issue at a time: *"Let's just talk about money right now. Then we can get to the kids."*

Sit down and talk quietly: *"I better sit down and calm myself before we start talking."*

State your feelings clearly: *"When you yell at me, I feel hurt."*

Listen: *"I think I get your meaning. Let me repeat it to be sure."*

Be clear and specific: *"I can tell you exactly what I want you to do tomorrow at the bank."*

Stay flexible: *"I guess I'm being a little rigid now. Let me think about your idea."*

Be willing to negotiate and compromise: *"Okay, here's a possible compromise."*

Breathe calmly and stay relaxed: *"I better take a few deep breaths about now to stay relaxed."*

Take responsibility for everything you say and do: *"I said it, so I can't just take it back like the words never came out."*

Focus on solutions, not victories and defeats: *"Let's find a way for both of us to be happy about this issue."*

Take time-outs as needed: *"I'm starting to get too emotional. I need a time-out."*

30: DEEP RESENTMENTS AND THE NEED TO FORGIVE

What to Know

Deep resentments develop when someone says or does something that seriously hurts you and the injury gets stuck in your head. You can't let go of it. Gradually it takes up more and more space in your mind until it completely colors the way you think about and act toward the offender. Ultimately, strong resentment can turn into hatred, which means you despise the person who harmed you. You've turned the other person into someone bad, evil, awful, beyond redemption.

Forgiveness is the key to ending a deep resentment. Forgiveness is an act of generosity on your part. It can never be earned by the offender. When you choose to forgive, you take the offender back into your heart by focusing on their humanity instead of on how they harmed you. Forgiveness is never fast or easy. But there are a few things that you can do to help you get a good start on the process.

What to Do

Make a clear and conscious decision to forgive.

Quit blaming the other person for your unhappiness.

Stop thinking about or doing anything in the name of revenge.

Let go of any demands you've made for an apology or other form of repayment. Basically, rip up the debts.

Think about some of the good things the offender has done.

Imagine what it would be like to allow this person back into your heart.

More to Know

Forgiveness is a long and slow process. That's because the offender has done things to you that have deeply wounded you. It's actually quite common to engage in several rounds of forgiveness. First you make a conscious effort to forgive and feel like you've succeeded, and then you experience a surge of the old anger and hostility toward the offender.

That's normal, so don't be discouraged. Forgiveness isn't an all-or-none event. It's more like a series of efforts in which you gradually achieve lasting peace of mind.

What if you're not ready to forgive? That's okay. Do not let anybody tell you that you must forgive the offender right now. Forgiveness often backfires when it is shoved at you. You'll know when you're ready. You'll hear a message coming from somewhere inside you that says it's time to forgive and get on with your life.

What if, though, you simply cannot forgive the offender? Maybe you've already tried and failed. More likely you get totally angry every time you think about this person. Even so, you have a couple options to keep the offender from having free rent in your brain. *Distraction* is one possibility. You can stay busy, make yourself think of other things, and generally get on with your life. The other choice is to set a goal of achieving *emotional indifference* toward the offense and offender, which means remembering what happened without getting all emotional about it.

One reason some people avoid working on forgiveness is that they mistakenly believe that forgiveness means getting back into a relationship with the offender. That's simply not true. You can forgive someone without reconciling. Perhaps a very good friend stole thousands of dollars from you because of a gambling problem. You can choose to forgive them without having to resume the friendship. Indeed, you'd be naive and gullible to let that person ever get near your wallet again. Of course, you might choose to become friends again, but only after they've done a lot to deal with their gambling problem. Reconciliation is built upon trust as well as forgiveness, so you won't want to reconcile until you have good reason to trust them once more.

More to Do

If forgiveness is not yet possible, then work on distraction or emotional indifference, so the offender stops taking up so much room in your mind. Or choose to forgive. Then take action to start moving that way.

31: ANGER-TURNED-INWARD AND SELF-FORGIVENESS CHALLENGES

What to Know

It's easy to recognize anger problems when someone directs their anger against others. It's harder to recognize anger you've directed toward yourself. This *anger turned inward* happens when you won't or can't forgive yourself. Anger against yourself often takes one of these forms:

Self-neglect: A good example of self-neglect is not bothering to make doctor appointments for yourself because you're too busy taking care of others. The message in self-neglect is that you believe that you're not worth caring about.

Self-sabotage: A way to ensure you don't succeed in life. You're sabotaging yourself when you pull defeat from the jaws of victory, finding creative ways to fail just before you would succeed at some task or goal.

Self-blame: You convict yourself of being responsible for anything bad that happens. It's as if you carry around a sign saying "I'm bad. I'm evil. I'm worthless."

Self-attack: You attack yourself by saying mean things about yourself to yourself or perhaps by physically harming your body.

Self-destruction: You believe that you must destroy yourself because of your intrinsic badness. An example is suicide attempts.

What to Do

How familiar are you with these five forms of anger turned inward? Can you think of recent examples in which you harmed yourself in one or more of these ways by turning your anger inward?

More to Know

Anger turned inward is most difficult to correct when it reflects your inability to forgive yourself.

Jerome, formerly a violent man, says he can never forgive himself for having beaten his children. Claudia, a recovering alcoholic, says she could never forgive herself for the years she neglected her children when she was in the midst of her addiction. Both of these people have changed, though. Neither is abusive or neglectful anymore. So why can't they forgive themselves and move on?

Self-forgiveness is difficult because unforgiving people are often haunted by guilt and shame. Guilt is about transgression, going too far, and violating another's rights. Shame is about failure, not going far enough, and falling short of your values and goals. You may be unable to forgive yourself because, like Jerome, you feel guilty for doing something bad to others or because, like Claudia, you feel ashamed that you didn't do something good. In reality, Jerome and Claudia probably feel both guilt and shame because the two are so easily intertwined.

The past infiltrates the present with thoughts like *I must keep punishing myself for having been such a horrible person.* It's not that *I was a bad person* so much as an underlying belief that *I still am a bad person.* To someone who cannot forgive themselves, the past is never actually in the past.

More to Do

So how can you put the past in the past where it belongs? One way is to create a ritual you can repeat regularly to yourself. This ritual follows a then-versus-now format.

Jerome's might look like this:

Then I hit the kids. Now I hug them.

Then I was proud of my toughness. Now I'm proud of my gentle spirit.

Then I was selfish and greedy. Now I try to be generous and thoughtful of others.

Here's Claudia's:

Then I neglected my kids. Now I take good care of them.

Then I drank myself stupid. Now I'm sober and smarter.

Then I fell short of my values. Now I'm living up to my goals and beliefs.

Accept what you did in the past while celebrating the good person you are today. Come up with your own then-versus-now statements to put the past in the past and embrace the person you've become.

PART 4

BEING GOOD TO YOURSELF

Anger can mask other feelings, but most often it is a response to pain (see chapter 23). Something feels very wrong, and anger seems like a way of coping with it. Whether the distress is emotional or physical, for a moment the anger masks it.

This next part of the book is about dealing with your distress in proactive ways, so anger will be less and less needed in your life. It's about nourishing and being good to yourself. It's about creating a life where your physical and emotional well-being are high priorities.

32: TLC (TIRED, LONELY, CRAVING) ISSUES

What to Know

The first step in taking better care of yourself is learning to be more aware of what we call *TLC issues*:

Tired/stressed

Lonely

Craving (food, peace, stimulation, meaning...)

At least half of all anger episodes are in some way associated with TLC issues. It's far more effective to work on these issues directly, as a problem to solve, than to cover your distress with angry words. You'll end up feeling a lot better, and so will those around you.

What to Do

A simple but important discipline in anger control is to ask yourself, any time you're starting to get hot, *What's my TLC level?*

Here's how to further understand your TLC level. Ask yourself:

Am I tired or physically distressed in any way? Do I need to sit, take a break, sleep, relax my muscles?

Am I feeling a need for social contact? Would it help if I talked to someone right now? Or just spent time doing something fun with someone?

Am I hungry for something? Do I need food or quiet or something interesting to do?

Once you identify a TLC issue, shift the focus to what you can do about it. The road to anger is feeling stuck and helpless, so solving TLC distress is a high priority. Don't put it off if you can help it. Make a plan right away to get rest, contact a friend, or do something fun. If at all possible, plan to address a TLC issue on the same day you notice it.

That way to relief is in sight. You can look forward to feeling better rather than feeling helpless and angry.

33: PUT A CORK IN THE SELF-HATING VOICE

What to Know

People who struggle with anger often have strong judgments about others. But that gun points both ways. They frequently reserve the most negative, hateful judgments for themselves. This self-attacking voice has been called the *pathological critic*. It's usually a whole load of judgments you've internalized from things your parents, caregivers, peers, or someone else close to you said over and over. This inner critic calls you stupid, lazy, or selfish; it says you're ugly, crazy, incompetent, or boring.

Sometimes the pathological critic attacks you for a lot more than what others actually said. It condemns you for what their actions *suggest* they felt toward you. For example, if they paid you little attention and rarely helped when you needed it, this inner critic might say you are worthless or a burden to everyone.

The main function of the pathological critic is to keep you feeling as rotten as you did as a child, to keep that old negative identity intact. Its main weapon is a stream of vicious, negative labels. And the result is a hidden world of shame and self-contempt. In the end, you're in so much pain that the slightest hurt or criticism from others feels intolerable, and you fly into a rage.

So you see how the attacks of your pathological critic feed into your anger problem. The worse you feel about yourself, and the more shame and vulnerability you carry, the more likely you are to cope by using anger. Doing something about your anger requires that you also do something about the pathological critic and all its judgments.

What to Do

What are some negative thoughts you have about yourself? Are these thoughts feeding your pathological critic and your anger? What might it be like to counteract those negative thoughts with positive thoughts about yourself?

Think of three positive things about yourself and write them down, even if you don't think they're true. What does it feel like to have positive self-thoughts?

34: FIND CORE QUALITIES IN YOURSELF THAT YOU VALUE

What to Know

Deep down, you know there are good things inside you. You can draw on that for ammunition to fight your inner critic. So it's time to find out more about some of your positive core qualities and explore what's good about yourself.

What to Do

Take inventory of your core qualities. Complete the following prompts in a notebook or journal, using brief descriptions of each quality.

1. What qualities in you have others praised and appreciated?

2. What qualities does the person who loves (or who loved) you most appreciate?

3. What qualities helped you survive life's struggles, pain, and dangers?

4. What qualities helped you reach certain life goals?

5. What qualities allow you to help or bring happiness to others?

6. What qualities at times help you feel happy, proud, or good about yourself?

Now name some things you're good at in any of these areas:

- With your romantic partner, a close friend, or family member…

- With your children, nieces, nephews, kids of friends…

- At work, school…

- Sports, hobbies, recreation…

- Creativity, crafts, art, music…

- Taking care of your home, your garden…

- Taking care of yourself…

Now carefully review the list of personal qualities you identified in this exercise. Write down the top three qualities you value most and feel best about. When you feel your inner critic talking you down, remind yourself of these core qualities about yourself instead of listening to the critic.

More to Know

Often, it isn't enough to simply recognize positive qualities in yourself. You must actively work to keep them in mind. One strategy for increasing awareness of core qualities is called *active integration*. This involves regularly looking for past examples of your positive qualities in action. Here's how Jasmine, an out-of-work accountant, used active integration for three of her core qualities.

Day 1:

Quality 1: Caring. *I visited my grandmother daily when she was in the hospital last spring.*

Quality 2: Taking risks. *The time I asked Devon out, even though I'd just met him in a supermarket.*

Quality 3: Being lighthearted. *I kind of make people feel more up, like getting everybody laughing at Lisa's birthday party.*

Day 2:

Quality 1: Caring. *When I went right over to Gabriel's house to comfort him after his mother announced she was divorcing his dad.*

Quality 2: Taking risks. *I told my boss about some problems with his leadership style.*

Quality 3: Being lighthearted. *Even after that skiing accident, I was still joking with everyone and not getting all down about it.*

More to Do

Recall some different examples of your top three positive core qualities. Do this every day for up to a week. Then move on to three other positive core qualities from your inventory, and do the same.

After another week of recording examples of your core qualities in action, write a summary of the main positive qualities you've uncovered. Include some of the situations or relationships where that quality has shined. Jasmine's core qualities summary looked like this: "I'm a sunny, lighthearted person who cheers people around me. I'm supportive and caring, particularly when people are sick or hurting. I give people courage when they're scared, and I show them how to face situations through my own example. I take risks to achieve goals. I'm a good athlete, an honest and loyal friend, and a terrific (as yet unpublished) writer of children's stories."

Read your core qualities summary every morning. Make it part of your daily routine so that the words become incredibly familiar or you even know them by heart. The idea is to use the summary as an affirmation of qualities that you need to remember and cherish in yourself.

35: PRACTICE ACCEPTANCE

What to Know

The key to self-acceptance is to recognize that you're doing the best you can. This is hard to remember sometimes because your inner critic would rather have you believe that you are willfully screwing up, making one deliberate mistake after another. The facts are quite different. If you were to go back with an open mind to explore the actual process by which you made a regrettable decision, you'd find that you made the choice that seemed best at the time.

Your needs, fears, stresses, personal history, and a host of other factors influence your behavior and choices in any given moment. At the moment a choice is made, it feels right. It feels like the thing you have to do. You may have doubts, but you go ahead, hoping and expecting that things will turn out okay. Accepting this will quiet that inner critic's voice.

What to Do

There's a simple way to prove that you're doing the best you can. Think back to something you did that really angered another person and that you regret. Now write down how the following influenced your behavior and choices:

1. Your needs at that moment

2. Your fears at that moment

3. Your pain or stress at that moment

4. Any personal history or experiences that influenced your behavior or choices

5. What you knew or didn't know at the time

6. Your skills or lack of skills that influenced your choice at the time

7. Any physical or emotional limitations that influenced you to act as you did

8. Personal values or beliefs that influenced your behavior

9. The prospects for rewards or pleasures that influenced your choice at that moment

10. Resources that you did or didn't have at that moment that influenced your choice

After working through this exercise, is it clear that your behavior seemed the best available choice at the time? You might, with hindsight, do something different if the choice came up again. But your response appeared to be the best one when you made it.

If you are still uncertain that you make the best choices available to you (even though they may sometimes anger others), do the exercise with another situation or two. Or alternatively, try doing this exercise for a situation in which you were angry over another person's choice, and try to identify the main influences on their behavior.

You will greatly reduce your anger response when you can accept that we are all doing the best we can to take care of ourselves.

More to Do

Part of accepting your experience is revising negative labels with alternative thinking. Think back over the past few months to times when you felt particularly down on yourself. What was your inner critic telling you? What pejorative word or phrase did the critic use to describe your behavior? Write down all the negative labels your critic slings at you: ugly, dumb, loser...

It's time to revise some of these hurtful labels. First of all, these labels are far too global. In truth, how often do you behave this way? Once a week? Once a month? Once in a lifetime? What exactly is the problem or undesirable behavior? Describe it specifically in your journal.

If, for example, the label is "stupid," how often do you act this way? What exactly, behaviorally, does "stupid" mean? That you forgot the PTA meeting twice in the last year? That you confided to a friend about a problem that you wish you'd kept to yourself? The point is to define carefully what these negative evaluations are supposed to be describing.

Now, note any balancing realities: positive things you do that counterweight the negative. For example, you're often awkward in conversation with strangers but are warm and engaging with friends. Or you have several nasty fights a year with your mother but are faithful about calls and visits. Write these positive things down.

Here's an example of what Jasmine's list looked like:

Negative labeling: *Foolish and impulsive*

Alternative thinking: *Basically, this means I bought several outfits I shouldn't have for about $350 total. On the other hand, I'm paying the card down and looked great at the reunion.*

Negative labeling: *Stupid*

Alternative thinking: *I got in trouble three times at my last job for math mistakes, but they also said I had a good knowledge of tax law.*

Negative labeling: *Self-centered bitch (my brother's line)*

Alternative thinking: *I think a lot about my appearance and my own needs. I am also generous with my time and lend my support to friends and family.*

From now on, any time you catch yourself using a negative label, challenge it. Turn it into a statement that's specific and accurate, and find other positive qualities that balance it.

36: NOURISH YOURSELF

What to Know

Nourishing yourself will improve your quality of life and help keep anger at bay. Actively combating stress in your life with self-nourishment will help you handle provocations in more effective ways.

There are three main components to self-nourishment: physical comfort, connectedness, and emotional balance. It's time to explore some new self-nourishment activities to include in your daily life.

What to Do

Take out your journal and write down any of these activities that you would like to do to improve your physical comfort, your connectedness, and your emotional balance.

Physical Comfort

Temperature/warmth: keeping room temperature optimal; taking a hot shower or a bath

Clothes: wearing pleasing texture and color; loose rather than constricting

Bed: getting good support; warm and comforting bedding

Furniture: having at least one good, comfortable chair; a work space with room to spread out

Food: eating healthy, good-tasting foods

Drink: warm or cool quenching beverages; avoiding caffeine

Massage/sensuality: experiencing relaxing physical touch

Tension level: doing relaxation exercises; meditation

Energy: getting rest, sleep, quiet time

Movement: doing aerobic exercises; stretching; athletics

Pain level: getting immediate treatment for pain, or something to soothe it, if possible

Smell: avoiding unpleasant odors; consider using scents

Grooming: getting manicure; getting a haircut

Pace of life: avoiding rushing; planning space between appointments and events; opting for generous deadlines

Connectedness

Friends: keeping up regular contact through phone calls and visits; planning shared activities

Groups: belonging to a regularly scheduled group activity, such as those related to sports, hobbies, political or community action, educational or creative groups

Family: having regular contact with supportive and interested family members

Generosity: giving to and doing things for others

Partner: creating time alone with each other; scheduling fun; planning sensual or sexual experiences; giving small gifts (either objects or your time and energy)

Community: participating in church activities, the PTA, town hall meetings, the neighborhood association

Emotional Balance

Meaning: setting and pursuing a goal; service to others; creating something

Pleasure: scheduling time for things you enjoy

Limits: saying no to things you don't want to do or experience

Gratitude: daily meditation on what you appreciate and value in your life

Mindfulness: disciplining your mind to focus on the moment, such as what it feels like to wash the dishes, drive with the window open, take long strides as you walk home; mindfulness meditation

Creativity: making things, whether poetry and art or hemming new curtains

Aesthetics: arranging your environment so there are more things you like to look at

Nature: planning regular visits, however brief, to your favorite natural environments

Learning: gaining new knowledge; developing a new skill

Affirmation: reminding yourself regularly of your positive core qualities

Time alone: scheduling private time to think, reflect, and plan

Stress breaks: scheduling brief recovery periods (from a few minutes to a few days) to help manage stressful situations

After work cooldown: time to decompress immediately after getting home

Passive relaxation: reading books, watching movies, attending plays

Active relaxation: pursuing hobbies, interests, personal projects

Review the notes you've made in your journal and choose three self-nourishment activities to try first. Next, make a self-nourishment plan. It's not enough to want to do something. You have to plan for it and integrate it into your life. You can find a downloadable worksheet to plan your self-nourishment activities at http://www.newharbinger.com/51338.

37: SELF-SOOTHING SKILLS

What to Know

Managing the aftermath of an anger episode is one of the most challenging and painful tasks involved in learning how to manage anger effectively. The aftereffects of anger—from the impact of this emotion on your energy levels and emotional and physical state to the consequences of things you said or did out of anger—tend to linger long after the initial emotion has passed. For these reasons it is helpful to know how to deal with the aftereffects.

One of the best ways to care for your body is to soothe yourself physically (Linehan 1993b, 2015). Self-soothing skills can help you replenish your body's resources and return to a calmer state. The physical toll of intense anger can put you on edge and leave you vulnerable to more intense anger or other emotions. Soothing yourself physically in the wake of intense anger can reduce your risk for both. Think of it as a prevention strategy: the quicker you can recover from an episode of intense anger, the less vulnerable you'll be to intense anger in the future.

The idea behind self-soothing skills is to introduce a comforting sensation to the five senses: touch, taste, smell, sight, and sound. The best self-soothing strategies are those that activate more than one sense at a time.

What to Do

See if you can come up with five self-soothing skills that will work for you by introducing one or more comforting sensations. Here are some suggestions. Choose any that appeal to you or choose another self-soothing activity that comes to mind.

Touch. Introduce sensations that soothe your body and feel good against your skin. Put on soft clothing, such as a fuzzy sweater, flannel shirt, cotton sweatshirt or T-shirt, warm fleece, or silk shirt. Focus on the feeling of the fabric against your skin. Take a warm bubble bath or hot shower, or sit in a hot tub. Focus on the feeling of the water against your skin. Sit in a sauna or relax in the sun, focusing on the warmth against your skin. Get a massage or give yourself a massage. Pet your cat or dog (or other animal), focusing on the feel of the fur against your skin. Hug a friend or loved one. Wrap yourself up in a warm, fluffy blanket and curl up on a comfortable chair or in bed. Sit in front of a fire and focus on the warmth you feel.

Taste. Eat your favorite comfort food, such as mashed potatoes, macaroni and cheese, cinnamon buns, sushi, or freshly baked bread. Sip a cup of hot cocoa or tea or some other hot drink. On a hot day, eat a popsicle or an ice cream bar. Eat dark chocolate or a piece of fresh fruit and focus on the flavors.

Smell. Burn incense or light a scented candle and focus on the scents that are released. Apply scented lotion to your skin and inhale the aroma. Go to a flower shop or botanical garden and breathe in the scents of the flowers. Inhale the aroma of lavender or vanilla. Go outside and breathe in fresh air. Bake cookies or bread and breathe in the aroma. Smell fresh coffee beans or brew coffee. Cut fresh herbs or open jars of spices and breathe in deeply. Light a fire and focus on the smell of the smoke and burning wood.

Sight. Look at pictures of loved ones or a favorite vacation spot. Look at pictures of things you find relaxing, such as a beach, a sunset, or a beautiful mountain. Go to the beach and watch the waves hit the sand. Watch a sunset. Watch clouds in the sky or leaves rustling in the breeze. Watch your pet or children play or sleep. Watch the flames of a fire or candle move and dance in the air.

Sound. Listen to relaxing music, birds singing, or children playing. Take a walk through the woods or around your neighborhood and listen to the sounds of nature. Sit outside at dusk and listen to the crickets. Go to the beach and listen to the sound of waves crashing on the shore. Light a fire and listen to the pop and crackle of the wood.

Once you've identified some self-soothing skills, it's time to put them to the test. The next time you're on the other side of an anger episode and notice that you feel depleted or on edge, try one of these skills to deal with these aftereffects.

When you practice these activities, be sure to focus your attention completely on your sensations. Stay in the moment. If you find yourself getting distracted, just notice it and then turn your attention back to your senses.

38: MANAGING GUILT

What to Know

As already noted, the things you do or say when you're intensely angry can have aftereffects. Facing the consequences of your anger actions and their impact on those you care about is both necessary and difficult. Even as you continue to practice the skills in this book, there will probably be times when you do or say things out of anger that you later regret. Therefore, it's important to learn skills for managing the negative consequences of harmful anger actions.

Doing something you regret is a recipe for all kinds of distressing and painful emotions. Two of the emotions people experience most frequently following ineffective or harmful anger actions are guilt and shame. Chapter 31 touched on both guilt and shame, and on the importance of self-forgiveness. This chapter will focus on guilt, which stems from your own negative evaluations of your behaviors or actions. Guilt can be a helpful emotion if it motivates you to not repeat certain behaviors or to repair the damage to relationships caused by your actions. Guilt about expressing anger ineffectively can motivate you to express anger differently in the future, to use skills to better manage your anger, or to apologize to the person you hurt. All of these can be helpful ways of managing the aftereffects of anger outbursts.

You can think of guilt as a signal to make amends for your behavior and to repair any relationships that were hurt as a result. Therefore, some of the most helpful skills for managing guilt involve acting on the emotion directly (Linehan 1993b, 2015).

What to Do

1. Acknowledge the negative consequences of your behaviors. It's hard to make amends without first acknowledging how your actions have negatively affected others. Therefore, doing so is the first step in managing guilt effectively. The next time you feel guilty about the ways you acted when angry, take some time to figure out the negative consequences of your actions for others.

2. Apologize. Once you've figured out how your actions hurt others, use that information to apologize for those actions (Linehan 1993b, 2015). Taking responsibility for your behavior, demonstrating that you are taking it seriously, expressing remorse for your actions, and saying you're sorry can go a long way in repairing any damage that was done. These actions demonstrate to others that you care about how your behaviors affected them.

3. Repair and strengthen the relationship. Repairing the relationships that were hurt by your actions is one of the best skills for managing guilt related to anger actions (Linehan 1993b, 2015). You can think of this skill as an extension of apologizing. Whereas apologizing helps get the relationship back to where it was before the anger actions, this skill involves working to get the relationship to a better, stronger place than where it started (Linehan 1993b, 2015). The next time you lash out at someone or act on anger in ways you regret, try to figure out what you can do to make the relationship even stronger than it was. Do something kind for the other person or go out of your way to bring them joy or pleasure. Think about what's

missing in the relationship and what would make it stronger. If you don't see them very often, plan an outing or get-together. If you've been distracted by the stress in your life, set aside time to focus all of your attention on the other person. Repairing and making the relationship stronger than it was is an excellent way to regulate guilt.

4. Let go of the guilt and move on. Once you've used your guilt to take responsibility for your actions, apologize, and repair the relationship, it's time to let go of the guilt and move forward (Linehan 1993b, 2015). You can think of this skill as the last step in managing guilt. As helpful as this emotion can be, it's only helpful when it motivates you to engage in positive behaviors. Once you've used your guilt in the ways detailed above, however, it has served its purpose. It isn't helpful if guilt hangs around after you've apologized and repaired your relationships. So once you've taken these steps to manage your guilt, it's time to forgive yourself and let go of this emotion.

39: MANAGING SHAME

What to Know

Shame is far less helpful than guilt. Rather than stemming from negative evaluations of specific things you said or did, shame stems from negative evaluations of yourself as a whole. As a result, shame leads to self-hatred and low self-worth (which are never useful!), and it can actually get in the way of changing problematic behaviors or making amends. Think about it. If you consider yourself to be a decent person who sometimes does things that aren't okay, you may experience guilt and may be motivated to change the behaviors you don't like. On the other hand, if you think you're a terrible person all around, it's probably hard to imagine that things could ever change. When you feel shame, it's easy to believe that it's pointless to work on changing your behavior. Because guilt and shame are such different emotions, the skills for managing them are different too.

What to Do

Objectively label your experience. One way to decrease shame is to use the mindfulness skill of objectively labeling your experience (Linehan 1993b, 2015) to stick to the facts of what happened. You used this skill in chapter 11 to identify your anger cues. You can also use this skill to help you describe yourself or your behaviors without judgmental or inflammatory language, such as "evil" or "horrible." Instead, describe in an objective way what you did when you were angry and what the consequences were. This skill will minimize self-judgments and the feelings of shame that go along with these judgments. Labeling your experience objectively will also allow you to focus on more productive and helpful responses, such as what you can do to repair the relationships that were damaged, or skills you can use to manage your anger more effectively in the future.

Act opposite to shame action urges. Another skill that can be helpful for managing shame is opposite action (Linehan 1993b, 2015). Chapter 3 focused on ways you can use the skill of opposite action to regulate ineffective anger. The same principles apply here. One way to modulate emotions is to act in ways that are counter to the action urges that go along with the emotion. For shame, the action urges are to hide, avoid, shut down, and self-punish. Therefore, if you want to reduce feelings of shame, the best strategy is to approach the people who were affected by your anger and use the skills discussed in chapter 38 to make amends and repair any damage that was done. Look them in the eye. Continue to reach out to others and surround yourself with people you care about. Do your best to avoid isolating yourself from others. As difficult as it may be to resist urges to avoid other people, doing so will help you reduce feelings of shame.

40: PRACTICING SELF-COMPASSION

What to Know

People who struggle with anger often have negative judgments about anger, which can cause them to judge themselves for experiencing it. Just the experience of anger itself—even if it is managed effectively and expressed skillfully—can result in self-judgments and shame. The problem with this is that anger is a normal, unavoidable human emotion. Therefore, beating yourself up or judging yourself as bad or evil for feeling anger isn't going to stop it from occurring. In fact, doing so will only make you feel worse. And anything that makes you feel worse and increases feelings of shame is only going to make you more vulnerable to intense anger in the future. Therefore, the next time you experience anger, it would be far better to treat yourself with compassion and kindness.

What to Do

Rather than beating yourself up for having a normal human emotion, treat yourself with love and respect. There are many ways to practice self-compassion.

Do something nice for yourself. Even if you don't feel loving toward yourself in the moment, you can behave lovingly by doing something nice for yourself. Give yourself a gift, treat yourself to your favorite meal or snack, watch your favorite television show or movie, or practice one of the self-soothing skills from chapter 37. Acting as if you love and respect yourself is one way to elicit those feelings and increase self-compassion.

Validate your anger. If you notice that you're judging yourself for feeling anger, shift your attention to the information your anger provided you. Remind yourself that all emotions—including anger—are valid and important and serve a purpose. Figure out what your anger was telling you and the purpose it served. Approach your anger as a friend or helpful guide rather than an enemy. Although it's important to be aware of the downsides of some anger urges, it's equally important to respect your anger and the benefits it can have.

Focus on your strengths and positive characteristics. Self-judgments can quickly take on a life of their own and spiral out of control. Although you may begin by judging yourself for experiencing anger, before you know it you may be judging yourself for all sorts of emotions and behaviors. Focusing on your positive behaviors and the things you like about yourself can counteract this spiral. For example, focus on all of the things you do that result in positive consequences for others. Think about steps you've been taking to improve your life and gain more skills. Recognize your accomplishments. Focus on the parts of yourself that you appreciate. Focusing on your positive characteristics and strengths can be very encouraging and can motivate you to make important changes.

Choose self-compassion over self-judgment. Beating yourself up for feeling anger or expressing it ineffectively can be demoralizing, making it less likely that you'll take steps to change.

MOVING FORWARD

No matter how many skills you use or how effectively you use them, the aftereffects of intense anger tend to linger long after the emotion passes. From the toll that any intense emotion takes on the body to the guilt and shame you feel when you lash out at others or act on anger in ways you regret, the aftereffects of anger can be just as difficult to manage as the anger itself. That's why it's so important to know how to take care of yourself and your relationships in the aftermath of an anger episode.

Think of the skills you have learned in this book as a road map to treating yourself and others with kindness and respect. No matter what you do when you're angry or how guilty you feel, beating yourself up is only going to make things worse. So have compassion for yourself. Recognize the effort you're putting into learning how to manage your anger more effectively. Give yourself credit for reading this book, learning about your anger, and practicing the skills you've learned here. Focus on the progress you've made and the ways your life will improve if you continue to work on your anger. And, when you do act out of anger in hurtful or ineffective ways, take responsibility for your actions, apologize for your behavior, and focus on improving your relationships and making them stronger.

Managing your anger more effectively will allow you to live life with fewer regrets and do more of what you want to do with your time and energy. Engaging in what matters helps make life meaningful, and this, in turn, is a path to greater emotional well-being and health (Costin and Vignoles 2020).

What are these things that matter most to you? For some, family and friends matter most. Others dive into areas of personal interest when they can. Some take time to defend those who can't protect themselves. For others, multiple things matter, such as writing stories, creating gardens, and restoring old stuff. Some build businesses. For some rare folk, their work is their magnificent obsession.

The next time you head toward an anger mindset about an event, pause. What are you grateful for having as a part of your life? Doesn't that matter more?

FURTHER READING

The Anger Control Workbook: Simple, Innovative Techniques for Managing Anger and Developing Healthier Ways of Relating by Matthew McKay and Peter Rogers

The Cognitive Behavioral Workbook for Anger: A Step-by-Step Program for Success by William J. Knaus

Thirty-Minute Therapy for Anger: Everything You Need to Know in the Least Amount of Time by Ronald T. Potter-Efron and Patricia S. Potter-Efron

The Dialectical Behavior Therapy Skills Workbook for Anger: Using DBT Mindfulness and Emotion Regulation Skills to Manage Anger by Alexander L. Chapman and Kim L. Gratz

The ACT Workbook for Anger: Manage Emotions and Take Back Your Life with Acceptance and Commitment Therapy by Robyn D. Walser and Manuela O'Connell

Instant Anger Management: Quick and Simple CBT Strategies to Defuse Anger on the Spot by Aaron Karmin

Thoughts and Feelings: Taking Control of Your Moods and Your Life by Matthew McKay, Martha Davis, and Patrick Fanning

Mind Over Mood: Change How You Feel by Changing the Way You Think by Dennis Greenberger and Christine A. Pedesky

Feeling Good: The New Mood Therapy by David D. Burns

REFERENCES

Costin, V., and V. L. Vignoles. 2020. "Meaning Is About Mattering: Evaluating Coherence, Purpose, and Existential Mattering as Precursors of Meaning in Life Judgments." *Journal of Personality and Social Psychology* 118 (4): 864–84.

De Couck, M., R. Caers, L. Musch, J. Fliegauf, A. Giangreco, and Y. Gidron. 2019. "How Breathing Can Help You Make Better Decisions: Two Studies on the Effects of Breathing Patterns on Heart Rate Variability and Decision-Making in Business Cases." *International Journal of Psychophysiology* 139: 1–9.

Linehan, M. M. 1993a. *Cognitive-Behavioral Treatment of Borderline Personality Disorder.* New York: Guilford Press.

————. 1993b. *Skills Training Manual for Treating Borderline Personality Disorder.* New York: Guilford Press.

————. 2015. *DBT Skills Training Manual.* 2nd ed. New York: Guilford Press.

Perciavalle, V., M. Blandini, P. Fecarotta, A. Buscemi, D. Di Corrado, L. Bertolo, F. Fichera, and M. Coco. 2017. "The Role of Deep Breathing on Stress." *Neurological Sciences* 38 (3): 451–58.

Matthew McKay, PhD, is a professor at the Wright Institute in Berkeley, CA. He has authored and coauthored numerous self-help books, including *The Dialectical Behavior Therapy Skills Workbook*, *Self-Esteem*, and *Couple Skills*, which have sold more than four million copies combined. He received his PhD in clinical psychology from the California School of Professional Psychology, and specializes in the cognitive behavioral treatment of anxiety and depression.

Peter Rogers, PhD, (1941–2004), was administrative director of Haight Ashbury Psychological Services. He coauthored *When Anger Hurts*, *The Divorce Book*, *The Anger Control Workbook*, and *The Community Building Companion*.

Ronald T. Potter-Efron, MSW, PhD, is a psychotherapist in private practice in Eau Claire, WI; who specializes in anger management, mental health counseling, and the treatment of addictions. He is author of *Angry All the Time* and *Stop the Anger Now*, and coauthor of *The Secret Message of Shame*.

Patricia S. Potter-Efron, MS, is a clinical psychotherapist at First Things First Counseling Center in Eau Claire, WI. She is coauthor of *Letting Go of Shame* and *The Secret Message of Shame*, as well as several professional books on anger and shame.

William J. Knaus, EdD, is a licensed psychologist with more than forty-six years of clinical experience working with people suffering from anxiety, depression, and procrastination. He has appeared on numerous regional and national television shows, including *The Today Show*, and more than one hundred radio shows. His ideas have appeared in national magazines such as *U.S. News & World Report* and *Good Housekeeping*, and major newspapers such as *The Washington Post* and the *Chicago Tribune*. He is one of the original directors of postdoctoral psychotherapy training in rational emotive behavior therapy (REBT). Knaus is author or coauthor of more than twenty-five books, including *The Cognitive Behavioral Workbook for Anxiety*, *The Cognitive Behavioral Workbook for Depression*, and *The Procrastination Workbook*.

Alexander L. Chapman, PhD, RPsych, is professor and coordinator of the clinical science area in the psychology department at Simon Fraser University in Canada, as well as a registered psychologist and president of the DBT Centre of Vancouver. Chapman directs the Personality and Emotion Research and Treatment laboratory, where he studies the role of emotion regulation in borderline personality disorder (BPD), self-harm, impulsivity, as well as other related issues. His research is currently funded by major grants from the Canadian Institutes of Health Research. Chapman has received the Young Investigator's Award from the National Education Alliance for Borderline Personality Disorder (NEABDP), the Canadian Psychological Association's Scientist Practitioner Early Career Award, and a Career Investigator award from the Michael Smith Foundation for Health Research. He has coauthored ten books, three of which received the 2012 Association for Behavioral and Cognitive Therapies' Self-Help Book Seal of Merit Award. Board certified in cognitive behavioral therapy (CBT) (Canadian Association for Cognitive and Behavioral Therapies) and dialectical behavior therapy (DBT) (DBT®-Linehan Board of Certification), Chapman cofounded a large psychology practice, and regularly gives workshops and presentations to clinicians and community groups both nationally and internationally. He also has been practicing martial arts, Zen, and mindfulness meditation for many years, and enjoys cooking, hiking, skiing, and spending time with his wife and sons.

Kim L. Gratz, PhD, is professor and chair of the department of psychology at the University of Toledo. Gratz directs the Personality and Emotion Research and Treatment laboratory, in which she conducts laboratory and treatment outcome research focused on the role of emotion dysregulation in the pathogenesis and treatment of BPD, self-injury, and other risky behaviors. Gratz has received multiple awards for her research on personality disorders, including the Young Investigator's Award from the NEABPD in 2005, and the Mid-Career Investigator Award from the North American Society for the Study of Personality Disorders in 2015. She has been continuously funded since 2003 (with continuous federal funding as principal investigator since 2008), and has authored more than 145 peer-reviewed publications and six books on BPD, self-injury, and DBT.

Real change *is* possible

For more than forty-five years, New Harbinger has published proven-effective self-help books and pioneering workbooks to help readers of all ages and backgrounds improve mental health and well-being, and achieve lasting personal growth. In addition, our spirituality books offer profound guidance for deepening awareness and cultivating healing, self-discovery, and fulfillment.

Founded by psychologist Matthew McKay and Patrick Fanning, New Harbinger is proud to be an independent, employee-owned company. Our books reflect our core values of integrity, innovation, commitment, sustainability, compassion, and trust. Written by leaders in the field and recommended by therapists worldwide, New Harbinger books are practical, accessible, and provide real tools for real change.

 **newharbinger**publications

MORE from
NEW HARBINGER PUBLICATIONS

**THE ANXIETY
FIRST AID KIT**

Quick Tools for Extreme,
Uncertain Times

978-1684038480 / US $16.95

**THE DEPRESSION
TOOLKIT**

Quick Relief to Improve
Mood, Increase Motivation,
and Feel Better Now

978-1648480065 / US $16.95

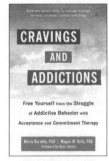

**CRAVINGS AND
ADDICTIONS**

Free Yourself from the Struggle of
Addictive Behavior with Acceptance
and Commitment Therapy

978-1684038336 / US $17.95

**A MINDFULNESS-BASED
STRESS REDUCTION
CARD DECK**

978-1684037797 / US $19.95

**ADULT SURVIVORS OF
TOXIC FAMILY MEMBERS**

Tools to Maintain Boundaries,
Deal with Criticism, and
Heal from Shame
After Ties Have Been Cut

978-1684039289 / US $17.95

**THE PAIN MANAGEMENT
WORKBOOK**

Powerful CBT and Mindfulness
Skills to Take Control of Pain and
Reclaim Your Life

978-168403644w8 / US $24.95

new**harbinger**publications
1-800-748-6273 / newharbinger.com

(VISA, MC, AMEX / prices subject to change without notice)
Follow Us

Don't miss out on new books from New Harbinger.
Subscribe to our email list at **newharbinger.com/subscribe**

Did you know there are **free tools** you can download for this book?

Free tools are things like **worksheets**, **guided meditation exercises**, and **more** that will help you get the most out of your book.

You can download free tools for this book—whether you bought or borrowed it, in any format, from any source—from the New Harbinger website. All you need is a NewHarbinger.com account. Just use the URL provided in this book to view the free tools that are available for it. Then, click on the "download" button for the free tool you want, and follow the prompts that appear to log in to your NewHarbinger.com account and download the material.

You can also save the free tools for this book to your **Free Tools Library** so you can access them again anytime, just by logging in to your account! Just look for this button on the book's free tools page. ➤ **+ Save this to my free tools library**

If you need help accessing or downloading free tools, visit **newharbinger.com/faq** or contact us at **customerservice@newharbinger.com**.